Desire and Fate

David Rieff

Desire and Fate

With a Foreword by John Banville

ERIS

ERIS

265 Riverside Drive
New York, NY 10025

86–90 Paul Street
London EC2A 4NE

ISBN 978-1-912475-38-4

Cover design: László Moholy-Nagy, *Structure of the World*, *c.*1925, gelatin silver print, 32.2 × 23.5 cm, © 2024 Artists Rights Society (ARS), New York / VG Bild-Kunst, Bonn

eris.press

Foreword

by John Banville

An Irish friend, let us call him 'A.,' spent the months of October and November 2016, in the United States, as a visiting something-or-other at one of the great Midwestern universities. He had been traveling to the US since the 1960s, and knew the country well; the East and the West coasts, of course, but, more to the point, that vast sprawl of land that lies between, which most coasters fly over without giving a first, never mind a second thought. However, A. had a deep fondness for and appreciation of the Midwest, not least because his wife was born in St Louis, and still had family there.

But from the moment in 2016 when he stepped off the plane into glorious autumnal weather, A. knew he had arrived in a land changed from the one he used to know. On the way in from the airport, his taxi passed by a stationary line of traffic, and he witnessed a driver get out of his car, red-faced and with his fists clenched, and stride back past six vehicles in order to deliver a violent kick to the driver's door of the seventh. It was for A. an emblematic moment. On the freeways, in the streets, in bars and restaurants, and even in private houses, every other person seemed to be in a fury. About what? Nothing, mostly.

That evening, on the phone, A.'s wife told him that her favourite aunt, who lives in Memphis, was going to vote for Trump. When she asked why, the old lady said she was for Mr. T. because he was going to bring down the whole rotten system. His wife was baffled—why would her aunt, an ex-teacher and solidly middle class, want to harm America? "Pah!" Said the aunt, "what did America ever do for me?" "Well," A.'s wife said, "you have a five-bedroom house, two cars, and a camper, and your three grown children have good jobs with good incomes." What more would she expect?

"Yeah, well," the aunt said bitterly, and hung up.

It was a response that A. was to hear frequently over the ensuing weeks. He was baffled. "You are so prosperous," he would say, "you have so much, and yet you're so angry." And promptly would come the familiar snarl: "Yeah, well."

Boredom, and the fear of it, A. had always held, is one of the strongest though largely unacknowledged forces in the lives of people. And America, he decided now, was deeply, perhaps terminally, bored.

He had lodgings in a pleasant house in one of the leafy suburbs surrounding the college campus. Some days after he moved in he was invited to dinner by a couple of hospitable academics to whom he had lately been introduced. They lived close enough for him to walk to their house. He set off, and at the first corner came upon a black woman, got up in what looked to him like a police uniform, pacing slowly up and down beside a telephone stand. They exchanged friendly greetings, and he stopped to chat.

She told him that one night a year or two previously a student in the area had been murdered by a mugger. There was an understandable outcry and, in response, the university authorities had set up emergency telephones at the corner of every block, each phone to be tended by a security guard. She was such a guard, and this was her beat.

How long was her shift? Ten hours a night. Did she get breaks? Yes: one of twenty minutes, and two of ten each. What did she do during her breaks? "I stand in that doorway over there." Did she have headphones, could she play music, or the radio? Nope—had to listen for the phone to ring, "which it never does," she said with a shrug.

"And what do you do in the winter?" He asked. Another shrug. "I get real cold."

"May I ask," he probed, "what you're paid?"

"Huh—peanuts."

Later on, over dinner at the luxurious ten-room apartment of the *bien pensant* couple, A. described his encounter with the security guard, and expressed his indignation that a person, *any* person, should have to do such a horrible, demeaning, and pointless job and be paid below the national basic wage.

The couple tut-tutted, shook their heads, murmuring sympathetic sentiments. Then, after a brief silence, the host brightened, and poured a glass of wine and pushed it across the table to A., saying, "Try this chardonnay, it's from the Napa Valley—I think you'll like it."

That was the moment, A. later recalled, when he knew without a shadow of a doubt that Donald Trump would be the next President of the United States.

In *Desire and Fate*, a dazzling and devastating critique of what in the English-speaking world goes under the label 'Woke,' David Rieff makes the point—and he makes it more than once, for emphasis—that the commissars of Woke culture are blithely indifferent to the politics of class. At the outset he writes:

> The Woke may or may not be getting wonkier, but the rich certainly are getting richer—a lot richer, in fact. This is how you can square what at first appears to be a circle: the demonization of traditional Western high culture and the most permissive attitude imaginable to the inequalities of class.

When did it all start to go wrong? A long, long time ago. Rieff cites an essay by the sociologist Daniel Bell published in 1970 entitled "The Cultural Contradictions of Capitalism," in which Bell argued that the traditional bourgeois value system was broken by the bourgeois economic system—"the free market, to be precise." Rieff has the highest regard for Bell, but contends that what he failed to see was that, while arts and artists in the West, certainly from the mid-nineteenth century onwards, "construed themselves as having as their mission the dissolution of the social status quo," in fact their real role "was to serve as a kind of inadvertent avant-garde of the free market by systematically destroying once and for all the Protestant Ethic."

Bell felt that what he saw as capitalism's new 'voluptuary system' of 'social permissiveness and libertinism' was not sustainable. Rieff agrees that "any social system needs some kind of moral warrant."

But in 1970, the year that ushered in the 'Me decade,' it was hard to see what that would be. Rieff writes:

> Half a century later, though, we know what it is: Woke, Critical Race Theory, Intersectionality, LGBTQ+, and the rest. These doctrines have moralized the voluptuary system, disciplined the libertinism, and politicized the permissiveness.

What these new pieties have established, in our post-religious age, is the cult of cults and the triumph of Kitsch, "which is the only kind of culture the free market can really tolerate."

Desire and Fate is a sustained, cogent, and brilliantly argued onslaught upon the current orthodoxies which hold sway particularly in the academic world, among arts funders, and in Silicon Valley.

Those readers old enough to remember the 1960s are these days surely experiencing a dispiriting sense of déjà vu. Back then, the academy gave in to the New Barbarism, which allowed the young of the middle class to indulge in a few years of hedonism, before putting on a suit and joining dad's stockbroking firm, or slipping into a designer dress and marrying, well, a stockbroker. Faux-radicalism then, like identity politics now, were, as Rieff says, "an uncommonly close fit" with capitalism.

The excesses and arrogant imbecilities which Rieff brings forward as evidence for the prosecution make for depressing, frightening, though sometimes hilarious, reading. "It seems obvious," he writes, "that we are entering full-speed a world whose good intentions will destroy what is good about this civilization without improving the many things that are cruel and monstrous about it."

In the newly awakened bourgeois world, Rieff argues, everyone is to be special, one is what one chooses to one be—so a nine-year-old boy can declare himself to be a girl and woe betide anyone who disagrees—and a reputable university press will publish Professor Leigh Claire La Berge's *Marx for Cats: A Radical Bestiary*, which, as the blurb-writer for Duke University Press has it, will identify "an animality at the heart of Marx's critique," since cats "have long been understood as creatures of economic critique and liberatory possibility."

Meanwhile a woman in a cheap uniform tends a public telephone for ten hours of a winter night, often in sub-zero temperatures. But no matter; as A. reports, yes, the chardonnay was very fine.

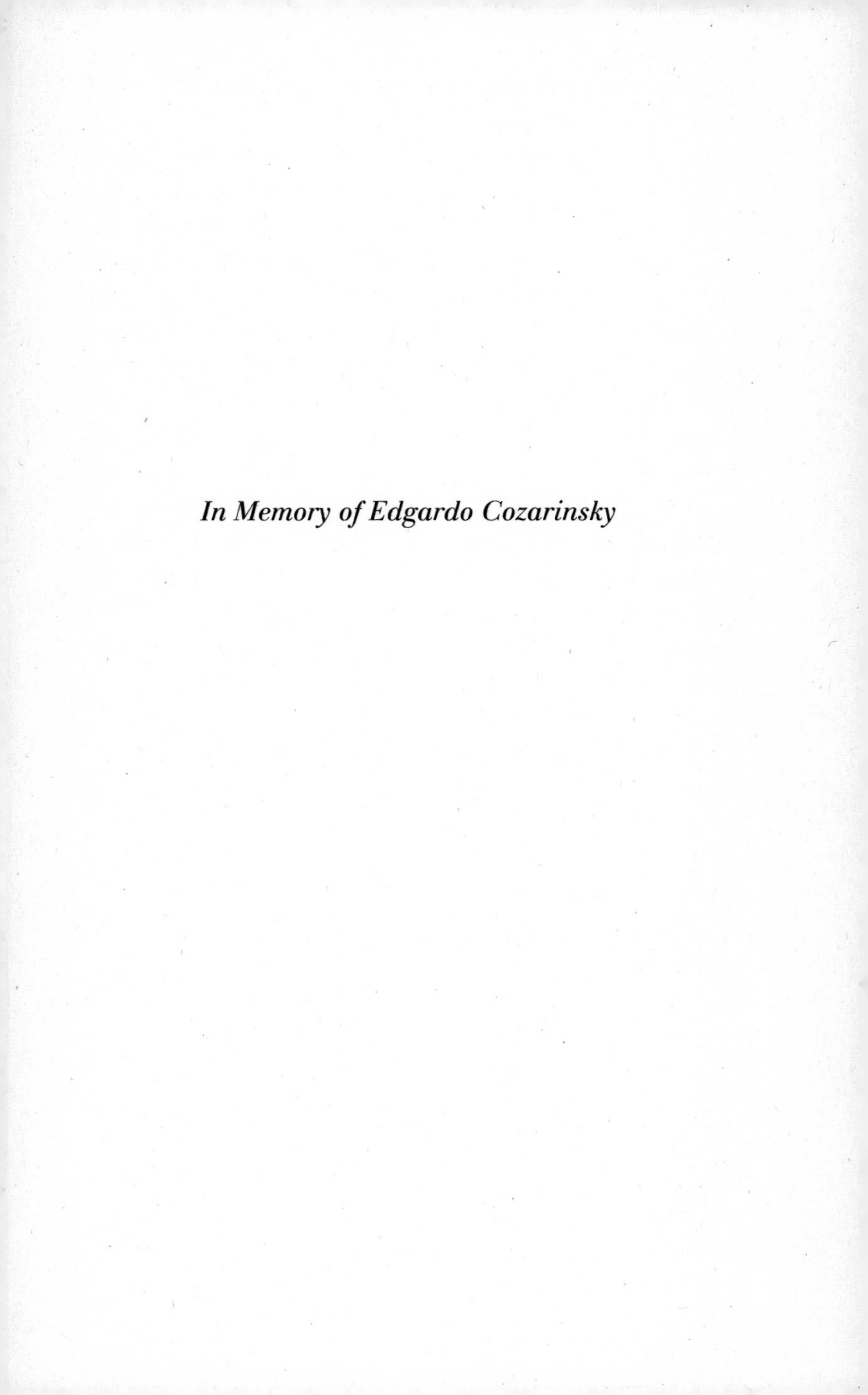

In Memory of Edgardo Cozarinsky

THE CULTURAL REVOLUTION that is sweeping across much of the rich world—with its mix of authoritarian subjectivity most radically expressed by the conviction that human beings are whatever they feel themselves to be and by a kind of lumpen Rousseauism in which what are now called 'indigenous ways of seeing' are taken to be at least reason's equal and, by many progressives, reason's superior—is without serious precedent. To be sure, many of its elements have obvious antecedents. Here are four of them: Communism's ambition to create a new kind of human being; the Chinese Cultural Revolution's demonization of the past yoked to an insistence that people express their repudiation of it publicly; the old European fantasy that pre-modern societies were fundamentally morally innocent; and the therapeutic revolution as it popularized (obviously, what Freud originally had in mind was something else entirely) and fetishized an imperial self that deserved fulfillment just because it was a self, and insisted that if the story one told about oneself couldn't be realized, then one had been cheated by one oppressive order or another.

What is new is the synthesis: two seemingly incompatible world views—radical individualism and the radical communitarianism we rather unsatisfactorily call 'identity politics'—easily coexisting within the same utopian narrative. But what also sets it apart is what—despite a certain amount of Marxist boilerplate that flies about in the academe—is its absolute intolerance of everything—White Supremacy, Patriarchy, heteronormativity, and so on—except for capitalism. As long as the business community doffs its cap to the new cultural dispensation—non-white people suddenly predominating in advertising, Pride flags at the entrances to the office towers of Fortune 500 companies—it can continue its merry way, as indeed it is doing. The Woke may or may not be getting wonkier, but the rich certainly are getting richer—a lot richer, in fact. This is how you can square what at first appears to be a circle: the demonization of traditional Western high culture and the most permissive attitude imaginable toward the inequalities of class.

This is a world in which it is deemed worse to be offended linguistically—misgendered, micro-aggressed, or traumatized by a book written in 1823 because it doesn't have the same attitudes as those in 2023—than to be deprived materially. What this means is that nothing in this cultural revolution will ever likely affect corporate bottom lines. The corporations understand this perfectly, of course, hence the velocity with which—much to the consternation of most of the political right—they tried on the motley of Woke and found it roomy and comfortable, and fits them very well. The only exception to this are the radical environmentalists. Their anti-capitalism is absolutely genuine, but that is because it is the anti-capitalism of fear. When these eco-warriors glue their hands to famous paintings, or throw soup over them, their *cri de coeur* is to wonder how can people care more about great art than the fact that the planet is burning. A Woke demonstration in a gallery with great Western paintings in it (though there would be no need for one, the curators would invite them with enthusiasm and excitement) would instead deprecate the art, highlighting its links to settler colonialism, the slave trade, and the rest. Today, the censor and the Bowdlerizer are home free.

And their audience, wallowing in the sheer deliciousness of their own performative virtue signaling, would be delighted—whereas when the radical Greens come calling, they are denounced as vandals.

As doubtless they are. But at least they are focused on their understanding, whether mistaken or not (in this context it makes no difference), of the factual realities of the climate crisis. They are hysterics of the fact. And the cultural revolutionaries? They are the hysterics of their feelings. In this age of punitive relativism, then, it should come as no surprise as to who is being tolerated, well-feted, indulged, and deferred to, and who is not.

UNSURPRISINGLY, THE DESTRUCTION that has taken place over the past quarter-century of the academic humanities in the name of equity, and the ease with which the identitarian requirements and interdicts of the academe—above all the insistence that representation is crucial, whereas quality is not—have prevailed in the corporate world across the Anglosphere, have caused many conservatives to reconsider their embrace of the so-called 'free market.' The obvious question is: why did it take them this long? Did they really not see that the capitalism with which they so identified—even allowing for the fact that this identification was in large measure dialectical, in the sense of their being pro-capitalist because they were anti-communist—was, as my mother once put it, "the bull in the china shop of human history"?

It is as if somehow conservatives imagined that the cultural worldview best expressed by T. S. Eliot in his "Tradition and the Individual Talent" (in which he argued that the true significance of an artist's work—even, indeed, perhaps especially, the work of the most innovatory and original artists, in the true rather than the gimmicky sense of this words (like Eliot himself)—lay in the relationship between that artist and the dead poets and artists who had come before) could long thrive in a capitalist culture.[1] Or, to put it another way, it is as if they somehow supposed that what Daniel Bell described as capitalism's "radical individualism in economics, and [its] willingness to tear up all traditional social relations in the process"[2]—an ideology that, to use the identitarian jargon of today, is by definition 'presentist,' and, more than that, is utterly disdainful of the past—could somehow still leave room for traditionalism in culture in the sense that Eliot meant.

For, tradition is, at least in the long run (since obviously there are always overlaps between historical and cultural eras), the cultural, and perhaps even the moral, opposite of innovation which, when all is said and done, is what the free market perpetually aspires to. To use the business school boilerplate, new technologies give rise to new industries, which in turn produce new goods and services. In the process, social relations are transformed. Even if those who believe that capitalism, through the process Schumpeter so famously described as "creative destruction," is the best economic system in history for creating prosperity, are correct, the price for that prosperity was always going to be high culture.

In his 1976 book, *The Cultural Contradictions of Capitalism*, Daniel Bell rejected Marx's idea that culture was a reflection of the economy, and was "integrally allied to it through the exchange process,"[3]arguing instead that culture had become ever more autonomous. And yet the connection Bell made between the growth of discretionary income, which had "allowed individuals to choose many varied items to exemplify a different consumption style," with an ever widening scope and reach of what he called "discretionary social behavior," and the advent of what he rightly considered to be a cultural order that proudly proclaimed itself the adversary of the established social order, actually fit in better with Marx's view than Bell's own, as evidenced by the fact that towards the end of his essay Bell concedes that,

> the breakup of the traditional bourgeois value system was, in fact, brought about by the bourgeois economic system—by the free market, to be precise.[4]

What Bell does not seem to have understood—and he did understand a great deal, much of which not only conservatives but liberals as well are only now coming around to understanding—is that while it is unquestionably the case that, at least from the middle of the nineteenth century forward—despite the presence of a few dissenting voices such as Eliot's—the arts in the West construed themselves as having as their mission the dissolution of the social status quo, with hindsight it is clear that their more important role in world historical terms was to serve as a kind of inadvertent avant-garde of the free market by systematically destroying once and for all the Protestant Ethic with all its moral and economic commitments to delayed gratification and to what Bell called "Malthusian prudence." Bell's language is elegiac. American capitalism, he writes, "has lost its legitimacy, which was based on a moral system of reward, and the Protestant sanctification of work." And writing in 1970, it is understandable that he thought that its replacement of Protestant moralism with hedonism, with what Bell called capitalism's new "voluptuary system" of "social permissiveness and libertinism," would be unsustainable.

And had it stopped there, perhaps Bell would have been right, since it is undeniable that any social system needs some kind of moral warrant, and in 1970 it was anything but clear what that new moral warrant would be. Half a century later, though, we now know what it is: Woke, Critical Race Theory, Intersectionality, LGTBQ+, and the rest. These doctrines have moralized the voluptuary system, disciplined the libertinism, and politicized the permissiveness. As for the cultural contradiction Bell warned of, that, too, has been settled, and in Carthaginian fashion, by the mechanism of condemning and repudiating the past as racist, which in practical terms means calling for the erasure of the high culture of the past. It could hardly be otherwise since historically high culture in every society has always been the product of the rich and powerful, of kings, empires, princes of religion, or plutocrats. And, thus, high culture became the only thing standing in the way of the free market, and now that too has been taken care of. Art can co-exist with Schlock, but it cannot indefinitely survive the onslaught of Kitsch, which is the only kind of culture the free market can really tolerate.

Schumpeter plus Fanon. Unimaginable. And, yet, once imagined, obvious; perhaps, even, inevitable. Because, at least in the long run, surely it is impossible to have an economic system based on obsolescence and destruction ('creative' or otherwise) and a cultural system based on pious continuity. We have moved from the Grand Inquisitor to the Grand Therapist.

ONLY EIGHT PERCENT of university students in the UK are enrolled in humanities subjects. This is the context in which the culture wars are being contested: as Borges said of the Falklands/Malvinas War, "it is a case of two bald men fighting over a comb." This does not mean the issues in dispute are unimportant; far from it. The madness of Woke and the barbarous inanities of 'anti-racism' are well on their way to destroying high culture in the Anglosphere and, probably, in parts of Latin America and Western Europe as well—even if in those regions there is the kind of cultural pushback that has all but disappeared in the Anglosphere. This is because most of the right in the US, Canada, and Australia is no more committed to high culture than it is to the preservation of the environment. In Western Europe and Latin America high culture has at least for a century not been a monopoly of the left—from Borges to Houellebecq, a conservative tradition remains alive. By contrast, in the Anglosphere, once one gets past Chesterton, Eliot, Flannery O'Connor, and Walker Percy, the cultural pickings are slim indeed.

For all that, however, in fifty years it is more likely that these culture wars will seem like the last spasms of a fish flapping desperately in its last moments on the deck of a fishing trawler, than it will the existential ideological and ethical conflict it so often appears to us today. Let us for once be honest: what is on offer in terms of contemporary culture on both sides of the Woke/anti-Woke battle line today is a penumbral shadow of the culture of the past. This is not to say that there aren't any people of talent in both camps. But, if we are being rigorous, it is simply a fact to say that the greatest days of Western culture are behind it. There is nothing unusual in this. Cultures and civilizations are as mortal as human beings. The great Renaissance historical and politician Francesco Guicciardini said that a citizen must not mourn the decline of their city. All cities decline, he writes. If there is anything to mourn it is that it has been one's unhappy fate to be born when one's city is in decline.

A lover of high culture should nonetheless be clear-eyed about the quality of what is being produced today. At its best it is good—not great. But a believer in the great Woke cultural revolution should be equally clear-eyed: the fantasy that culture can be largely a representation of the historically unrepresented, or that testimony is art, is a consoling fiction. In some ways, the Woke fantasy is a kind of infernal mix of Blake and Mao Tse-tung; the cult of experience fused with the cult of cultural revolution. At its worst, Woke culture is just Western fantasies about the authenticity and nobility of the tribal and the premodern; this in a time when racial identity has never been more in flux, and the intermingling of the races increasingly the norm (for the extreme end of this, look at who American Jews and Japanese-Americans marry). For "my race/people my spirit will speak," wrote the great Mexican thinker José Vasconcelos (it is hard to convey the exact meaning in English of the Spanish word 'raza'). But the Woke and the 'anti-racist' are tying themselves to the mast of an essentialist understanding of identity just as it is vanishing into air.

If there is a new culture waiting to be born, it will not be born of Woke and 'anti-racism,' of Neo-Tribalist nostalgia, and notions of race that, typologically

—though of course not hierarchically—would have pleased the worst of twentieth century White Supremacist scientist. But nor will Western high culture ever ascend to the heights that so many times, and so gloriously, it reached in the period between the Renaissance and the middle of the twentieth century. That race has run its course. And the point is that somewhere, deep down, everyone knows this. Given that, why in God's name would one want to study a subject in the humanities? There are, of course, material reasons for the death of the humanities as well. But one must be materialist, but not too materialist here; *allegro ma non troppo*, as it were. The old culture is dying, and what purports to be its successor has come into the world stillborn.

PEOPLE ON THE POLITICAL RIGHT (and not only on the right) still wax indignant about the speed with which capitalism seems not only to have capitulated to left identity politics but also to have enthusiastically incorporated it. Some view this as a betrayal, while more perceptive overseers on the right see the development as offering further proof of capitalism's skill at co-optation, and of its ability to neutralize movements in society that otherwise might be dangerous to it by, in effect, adopting a harmless version of it as their own—rather as is the case with vaccines, which use weakened or inactive parts of a particular organism (antigen) to trigger an immune response within the body. The assumption in capitalism's response to identity politics operates on the same principle: that such a weakened version will not cause the disease in the person receiving the vaccine, but it will prompt their immune system to respond much as it would have on its first reaction to the actual pathogen. And in both cases it has been remarkably successful.

In a capitalist society in which the ideal investment portfolio is 'diversified,' and the most effective business model is held to be one that 'disrupts' previous business models, it was always an absurdity to expect that on the commanding heights of cultural and intellectual life—which, for all its pretenses, are subordinate clauses in the economic sentence—'diversity' and 'disruption' would not soon come to be prized above all else. To be sure, there are other elements, above all the indifference of contemporary culture to tradition—at least, that is, to all tradition that cannot readily be monetized. But this, too, mirrors how irrelevant tradition is to contemporary capitalism—if not, indeed, to their immiscibility. This is the negative component. The positive, and far more important one, is that identity politics and contemporary capitalism are an uncommonly close fit. Think, for example, of the multiplication of identities in this culture, which are, to cultural and moral life, what market segmentation is to product portfolios. Or think of the way in which the humanities and social sciences are now devoted to repudiating the pasts of each of their disciplines and reimagining them—a 'verb,' by the way, that derives from the 'imagineers' of the Disney Corporation. Yes, within the academe the moral warrant for this is racism and other forms of exclusion. But the effect is the elevation of disruption to being the ideal state of cultural and intellectual life just as disruptive business models and new technologies that supersede their predecessors are the ideal state of a business enterprise.

For the left identarian, the past is something that needs to be transcended, not understood on its own terms, let alone honored (save for those who were its victims). Rather, to the extent it has any value as a field of study, it is only insofar as it can be recruited to the needs of the present. In university history departments this is explicitly referred to as 'presentism,' and those resisting it are fighting a doomed, rearguard action. But those who rightly oppose presentism—just as those in music departments who oppose the movement to deemphasize the Western classical tradition in favor of indigenous music or pop music, and those in classics departments who still resist the claim that their most important obligation is to teach the history of the marginalized not that of great men, and also imagine that these developments are somehow unrelated to the capitalist integument in which they are situated—badly misread what is taking place. Why teach about buggy whips when you can teach about virtual reality? And why imagine university students should be made to conform to university curricula, anymore than a consumer should—indeed, can—be made to accept a product not to their own liking?

In a capitalist world in which tradition is an impediment to profit, how could the culture that springs from it have any interest in honoring its own traditions? Yes, the identitarian left still largely proclaims to be, and for the most part genuinely imagines itself as being, anti-capitalist. But just as, in the old joke, the devil's greatest coup was persuading people he didn't exist, capitalism's greatest coup is making the cultural world believe it is autonomous of the market system—rather than being, like everything else, one of its many dependencies. To be clear, I have never doubted the sincerity of Woke. It is just that those who espouse it are vandals who mistake themselves for redeemers.

IN 1997, THE SOCIAL CRITIC Thomas Frank published an essay called "Why Johnny Can't Dissent."[1] In it, he argued that, over the course of four decades, the authentically countercultural ideas of the so-called 'Beat Generation' of the 1950s (of Jack Kerouac, Allen Ginsberg, and William Burroughs) that was "hostile to any law and every establishment," and consisted of what Frank called,

> a sort of Nietzschean antinomianism, an automatic questioning of rules, a rejection of whatever social prescriptions we've happened to inherit,

had become,

> capitalist orthodoxy, its hunger for transgression upon transgression now perfectly suited to an economic-cultural regime that runs on ever-faster cyclings of the new; its taste for self-fulfilment and its intolerance for the confines of tradition now permitting vast latitude in consuming practices and lifestyle experimentation.

The new capitalist dispensation, Frank argued, was dissent commodified and existential rebellion "more or less [having become] the official style of Information Age capitalism." And, once you commodify your dissent, he argued, it is no longer dissent in any serious—indeed, any credible—sense of the word. "In television commercials," he wrote,

> through which the new American businessman presents his visions and self-understanding to the public, perpetual revolution and the gospel of rule-breaking are the

orthodoxy of the day. You only need to watch for a few minutes before you see one of these slogans and understand the grip of antinomianism over the corporate mind.

And Frank went on to offer the following examples:

Sometimes You Gotta Break the Rules —*Burger King*
If You Don't Like the Rules, Change Them —WXRT-FM
The Rules Have Changed —*Dodge*
The Art of Changing —*Swatch*
There's no one way to do it. —*Levi's*
This is different. Different is good. —*Arby's*
Just Different From the Rest —*Special Export beer*
The Line Has Been Crossed:
The Revolutionary New Supra —*Toyota*
Resist the Usual
—*the slogan of both Clash Clear Malt and Young & Rubicam*
Innovate Don't Imitate —*Hugo Boss*
Chart Your Own Course —*Navigator Cologne*
It separates you from the crowd —*Vision Cologne*

In 1993, I had made a related argument in an essay in *Harper's Magazine* that identified capitalism as "multiculturalism's silent partner." What was surprising, I felt at the time, was that so many people who surely should have known better had they been willing to think coldly rather than sentimentally, had ever imagined there to be any necessary link between capitalism and Western culture. To the contrary, capitalism had always been "the bull in the china shop of human history," and the market economy—now global in scale—"by its nature corrosive of all established hierarchies and certainties, up to and including white racism and male domination." If any group had embraced the campus multiculturalist slogan, ""Hey, Hey, Ho, Ho, Western Culture's Got to Go," it was the world's business elite."[2]

The consternation of conservatives and of many mainstream liberals over the rise to cultural and institutional hegemony of Woke and Ibram X. Kendi/ Robin DiAngelo-style "anti-racism" has shown that the illusions of the 1990s about the supposed incompatibility of antinomianism and capitalism still persist to a remarkable degree. Obviously, some things have changed, most importantly the realization—particularly shocking to the political right across the Anglosphere—that capitalism can indeed be Woke. This has given rise to a revival on the right of a corporatist critique of capitalism not seen in the US since the 1930s—a critique that has provided the intellectual armature for conservative politicians to push back against this trend. Two notable examples of this are Florida's governor Ron DeSantis's attack on 'Woke corporations' like Disney, and the actions by a number of state treasurers in Republican-controlled states to withdraw billions of dollars of their states' monies invested in firms that subscribe to so-called ESG principles (the requirement that any prospective investment in corporations are conditioned on the latter's willingness to commit to various yardsticks related to social issues—above all of ethnic and gender 'diversity,' though, crucially, not of class—at the senior management and board level, and commitment to environmental action, such as reducing the corporations carbon footprint).[3]

But even this realization has largely come in the context of the belief that somehow capitalism has been 'captured' by Woke. For the former Levi's executive Jennifer Sey (whose memoir *Levi's Unbuttoned: The Woke Mob Took My Job But Gave Me My Voice* is a fairly representative example of the new genre of anti-Woke writing by figures within the business world) the crux of the problem is that too many CEOs quite simply "lack courage" and are "frauds" who "kowtow to the very vocal minority—the scant few employees marching outside of headquarters or emailing the head of Human Resources." Sey goes further in her book, claiming that, "Today's executives reared [their] kids with an 'I'm not your Dad, I'm your friend' parenting philosophy," and as a result are determined to "impress their Woke kids with their own progressive bona fides."[4]

A different, fundamentally moral, intellectual, and institutional explanation has been championed by the critic Wesley Yang, who has dubbed Woke "the successor ideology," by which he means the ideology that is replacing old school liberalism as a basic rubric for society across the Anglosphere.[5] But if the problem with Sey's view its that it is resolutely psychological, the problem with Yang's view is that it is resolutely conspiratorial. In a long interview he gave to Gerard Baker of *The Wall Street Journal* in 2022, Yang traced the beginning of the successor ideology to the mid-1980s[6] and,

> the first symposia on what was then called a new movement within legal academia called critical race theory. And critical race theory held that we must not take for

granted ideas of rationality, of free speech if we actually want to talk about obtaining reality in concrete terms in a society that has always been systemically racist and that continues to be systemically racist.

What followed, Yang argued, was,

> a long march through various institutions. It was not a march that I think the original founders anticipated would happen, but it happened in elementary schools. They captured schools of education. They captured schools of social work. They captured the discipline of psychology and so forth. And that long march to the institutions actually came to its fruition right around the year 2019 or 2020, because it was then that various school districts started to roll out a whole new curriculum that took as axiomatic these views that we can all be situated within a hierarchy of oppression, and showed the ways in which one is an oppressor, the ways in which another is oppressed, and it's then possible to tally these things up. We're going to engage in this exercise where we discover our intersectional identity and we're third graders. This is what we're going to do with our young people. And so the process of radicalization that happened spontaneously through Tumblr and within universities is slowly now in the process of being presented as axiomatic to a rising generation of Americans and to an already rising majority of Americans who are non-white.

Yang understands perfectly that this new successor ideology, far from being the inheritor of Marxism (despite much Neo-Marxist rhetoric from Woke ideologues within the cultural-philanthropic-academic complex), fundamentally diverges it from it by focusing on identarianism rather than the core conflict between capital and labor, and,

> doesn't seem to be in any way aimed at undermining or subverting the core capitalist relation. It just has redefined the utopia they have in mind as one in which there is proportional representation within the ownership class, within the upper reaches of the managerial classes of various identities.

As a result, Woke has,

> been very easily adopted by those who are at the commanding heights of our capitalist system. And so now we have Angela Davis giving a speech at Goldman Sachs. We have BlackRock and others engaged in the same annual, and it seems to take up an ever larger share of each year's calendar, of rainbow messaging and signaling of various kinds.[7]

Where I disagree fundamentally with Yang (as I venture to guess Thomas Frank would as well) is in his assumption that it took Woke to unseat old school liberalism. For old school liberalism had already been unseated by the transformations of capitalism that Frank and I identified in the 1990s. There was no need for any long march through the institutions because they had already changed out of all recognition with the bourgeois capitalism of which bourgeois liberalism formed, as a Marxist would say, the ideological superstructure. As Frank put it,

[t]oday corporate antinomianism is the emphatic message of nearly every new business text, continually escalating the corporate insurrection begun by [the American business guru, Tom] Peters. Capitalism, at least as it is envisioned by the best-selling management handbooks, is no longer about enforcing Order, but destroying it. 'Revolution,' once the totemic catchphrase of the counterculture, has become the totemic catchphrase of boomer-as-capitalist. The Information Age businessman holds inherited ideas and traditional practices not in reverence, but in high suspicion. Even reason itself is now found to be an enemy of true competitiveness, an out-of-date faculty to be scrupulously avoided by conscientious managers.[8]

In short, capitalism had already done Woke's and Critical Race Theory's work for them, so that by the time they arrived on the scene they were pushing on an open door. And the reason capitalism had had no qualms about opening that door for Woke and CRT was not just because, as Yang rightly understands and emphasizes, Woke poses no threat to capitalism, but because its antinomianism is as fully synergistic with the new antinomian capitalist order as liberalism—or, perhaps more accurately and less 'anglocentrically,' as social democracy was with the capitalist order of half a century ago. Above all, they share what Frank called "the imperative of endless difference."

This is not to say that there are not also fundamental differences between the antinomianism of the 1990s and that of today. Woke is tremendously Puritanical, its relation to pleasure willed rather than spontaneous, censorious more than accepting.

The extreme form of this can be found in the debates about sexual attraction that have arisen in the context of the mainstreaming of the trans movement. Where the students of 1993 in elite universities spoke of 'checking your privilege' (that is, recognize your favored and unearned status in your own society), students of today are likely to speak of 'checking your preferences,' or, sometimes, 'desirability politics,' by which they mean, for example, the question of whether you are being transphobic when refusing to date trans people, and should try to change this in yourself in much the way you can choose to renounce your class, gender, or race privileges. "Structural oppression," wrote Nancy Kelley, the chief executive of the British's largest LGBTQ+ campaign group, Stonewall, "can influence who we want."[9]

At its most extreme, this view—and while it is not commonplace in the trans world, it is certainly not *uncommon* either—entails insisting that what gender one identifies as is, or rather should be, dispositive, whereas one's genitalia should not. As the LGBTQ+ writer Layne Morgan put it on her X feed, "It's just harmful to trans folks to associate lesbian with 'vagina only' and gay with 'dick only' because gender ≠ genitals. Get it?"[10] But even less extreme versions of this view are actually very radical indeed, as is the case with the claim by the Oxford philosopher Amia Srinivasan that while,

> no one has a right to be desired, but also that who is desired and who isn't is a political question, a question usually answered by more general patterns of domination and exclusion.[11]

An even more important difference between 1990s antinomianism and our own is the centrality of the idea of trauma as a, if not *the*, central explanatory key not just to individual psychology, but to collective politics. Thomas Frank described commercial messages in the 1990s as having been driven home,

> with the vanguard iconography of the rebel: screaming guitars, whirling cameras, and startled old timers who, we predict, will become an increasingly indispensable prop as consumers require ever-greater assurances that, Yes! You are a rebel! Just look at how offended they are![12]

Today, however, in a society haunted by micro-aggressions and insistent on trigger warnings, where the collective trauma of racial and sexual minorities is taken for an indisputable fact, even though the evidence for this claim is at the very least more than open to question, the equivalent message would have to be: "Yes! You are a rebel! Just look at how offended *you* are!"

But in the main, there is more continuity than discontinuity between antinomianism 1.0 and 2.0. Two business books Frank pointed to, Charles Handy's *The Age of Unreason* (1989), and Michael Hammer's *Reengineering the Corporation: A Manifesto for Business Revolution* (1993), might as well be describing universities' humanities departments as successful corporations when, for example, Handy calls using new ways of "learning which can [...] be seen as disrespectful if not downright rebellious," and methods of approaching problems that have "never been popular with the upholders of continuity and of the status quo."[13] For his part, Hammer not only warned his readers in Corporate America to be suspicious of traditional practices, but argued that they needed to jettison pretty much everything their capitalist predecessors had believed since the time of Adam Smith and David Ricardo.

Today's antinomianism is, to be sure, more utopian, more repressive (particularly regarding issues of language), and more communitarian. But that beast slouching toward Bethlehem is recognizably the same. It is just that, instead of saying, "Commodify your dissent!" h..., s..., or...—go on, *you* pick your preferred pronoun—would also say, "Commodify your social justice!"

And they are busy doing it. An extreme example was the Kellogg Corporation's announcement (later retracted) that Pop, along with Snap and Crackle (the cartoon characters that have long been the 'mascots' of Kellogg's best-selling breakfast cereal Rice Krispies) is now "a trans woman." On X, a commentator asked in exasperation, "Can I eat my cereal in peace? Why does everything need to be a social justice campaign?"[14] In fact, there is a clear answer to that: because the risk of not *presenting* everything as a social justice campaign is that there will be a *real* social justice campaign, meaning one that might actually threaten the economic status quo in which corporate America has everything its own way in every essential sense. Take tax policy: in Kellogg's case, the massive government subsidies for high-fructose corn syrup that allow the company to price its breakfast cereals far below what they would have to charge were withdrawn; and in the power of corporate donations and corporate lobbying that has further corrupted and de-democratized an American polity that was already very corrupt and at best only partly democratic.

Once you commodify your dissent, Frank has argued, it is no longer dissent in any serious, indeed any credible, sense of the word. "In television commercials," he wrote,

> through which the new American businessman presents his visions and self-understanding to the public, perpetual revolution and the gospel of rule-breaking are the orthodoxy of the day. You only need to watch for a few minutes before you see one of these slogans and understand the grip of antinomianism over the corporate mind.[15]

The ironies! It is the right and not the left that wants to return Capitalism to its senses or, failing that, bring it to its knees, as one of the ablest right-wing activists, Christopher F. Rufo, has repeatedly said he thinks can happen with the Disney Corporation in the wake of Disney opposing the new Florida law that limits what teachers can say in classrooms about LGTBQ+ issues. The right is not wrong to see a Woke Disney. The company has adopted so-called 'inclusive language' at its theme parks so that visitors are greeted with a "Hello, friends," instead of "Hello, boys and girls." And one senior Disney executive, Karey Burke, confessed that, as the mother of one transgender child and one pansexual child she wants more gay lead characters in stories that aren't just about being gay, and has promised that a minimum of fifty percent of its characters will come from "underrepresented groups."[16]

Meanwhile, as long as these underrepresented groups are represented, the identarian left has little to say about the nature of Disney's product. Indeed, in many cases, this left and the ideologues of the so-called 'anti-racism' as preached by Kendi and DiAngelo are increasingly happy to become content providers for the corporate entertainment world. How far we have come from the 1970s and 80s when the Chilean writer Ariel Dorfman's book, *How to Read Donald Duck: Imperialist Ideology in the Disney Comic*, represented the left understanding of what companies like Disney were actually selling. Today, though, as long as it's inclusive and diverse—hey, what's the problem?

Thomas Frank predicted all this long before Woke:

> Contemporary corporate fantasy imagines a world of ceaseless, turbulent change, of centers that ecstatically fail to hold, of joyous extinction for the craven grey-flannel creature of the past.[17]

And, he added, while "the prominent culture warriors of the right might believe the counterculture was capitalism's undoing, the antinomian businessmen know better." Of course, in the twenty-five years since Frank published *Commodify Your Dissent*, counterculture has become *the* culture—period. To be sure, the antinomianism of the 2020s has a different specific gravity: it is no longer about the transgressive individual (individualism being as out of favor as liberalism or of class analysis) but rather about the transgressive group. It is this, I think, that explains the charisma that trans holds in the culture today, for it is that transgressive group *par excellence*.

What the right could not grasp then, and cannot grasp now, is that, on balance, antinomianism is good for business, at least in selected markets—though one imagines, that Disney will have to modify its content in China or in Saudi Arabia and the Gulf, and perhaps in Modi's India as well. But we know all about market segmentation. As for the left, none of this poses a serious problem, for there is no left militancy more provincial and self-involved than the identarian leftism of the Anglosphere. Ron DeSantis's anti-LGTBQ+ bill is an existential outrage, but China's mass imprisonment of the Uyghurs? No Disney 'creative' (to use the ghastly new word for writers, musicians, filmmakers, and animators) has called for a mass walkout to protest Disney's business in China, just as those calling for Netflix to sever its ties with the anti-Woke comedian Dave Chappelle, would try to mobilize against the infinitely more extreme misogyny and homophobia and transphobia of rap music.

A failure to contain inflation, a dramatic escalation of the war in Ukraine, a Chinese invasion of Taiwan, another pandemic, and climate change: these have the potential to threaten the capitalist order. Rice Krispies' Pop mascot being rebranded as a trans woman? That's just good business. If I am right, then the future of the Anglosphere is Capitalism With a Transgendered Face.

I MAKE NO APOLOGIES for discussing Woke in culture and the academe in ideological and moral terms, but one needs to be very careful in doing so not to divorce it from the material conditions in which it flourishes, and the larger institutional context in which it is situated. That context is one of universities increasingly being run on a business model where administrators' views have ever-increasing weight, and faculty views commensurately less. If you think of the university in that way, and of students as customers, then product innovation becomes important, especially in those disciplines where the financial rewards for studying them are paltry. Woke has provided this new product line and been able to present itself as offering moral improvement as an added benefit. If the humanities were a breakfast cereal company, they could advertise Woke as "Tastes Good" (translation: for the cereal's sugar rush, read: a lot less will be demanded of you in terms of knowledge) "And Is Good For You" (translation: you will be able to number yourself among the virtuous by immersing yourself in it).

At the same time, the conditions for humanities faculties are, increasingly, similar to those of the rest of the gig economy: with the graduate student teachers, teaching assistants, and non-tenure track instructors as intellectual Uber drivers. In this sense, the recent promising efforts at unionization are an emblem of the younger faculty's proletarianization in both financial and status terms. Think of the overqualified young people who work at Starbucks. And even if these efforts are successful, they will be so in an environment of ceaselessly diminishing employment prospects, as even the most cursory look at the numbers of humanities programs and their budget levels makes plain.

That's why I'm sceptical of the argument made most forcefully by Wesley Yang that Woke and the Kendi/DiAngelo version of 'anti-racism' can accurately be described as a 'successor ideology.' If anything, the reverse is the case: Woke is not only the emancipatory project of fools, to paraphrase August Bebel's celebrated line that Anti-Semitism was the Socialism of fools; it is a near perfect cultural superstructure for the capitalism of the contemporary Anglosphere—ostensibly caring; in reality utterly ruthless. The Woke academics can intone about racial capitalism all they like and denounce it from dawn to dusk. But that does not, and will never, make them anything other than its useful idiots.

THERE IS AN OLD JOKE in the intelligence services, that the ideal double agent is someone whom you recruit to betray their own countries by passing along to you their own government's most closely guarded secrets, but do so under the misapprehension that they work not for your agency but rather for the intelligence service of another country entirely. If caught, that double agent sooner or later will of course reveal everything about their treason. But if you work for the CIA but can successfully convince your mole that you are an agent of the Germany's BND, or France's DGSE (instead of for Langley), damage to your operation is unlikely to be anywhere near as bad as it would have been had your agent off the bat been able to tell the interrogators that it was the CIA that had been behind everything.

Looking at the eruption of Woke and the instauration of DEI and other Woke agendas begs the following question: is capitalism in the post-Protestant world engaged in similar manipulation? Obviously, the parallel is not an exact one. The CIA agent is trying to deceive the mole, whereas the corporate executives whose decisions are now partly shaped by that vulgarized version of Critical Race Theory peddled by Ibram X. Kendi and Robin DiAngelo are deceiving themselves. As for the university equivalents of the moles, there is no reason to doubt the sincerity of those espousing what has become the orthodox view in the academic-cultural-philanthropic complex that are at last shattering the bonds of White Supremacy, 'cishet' patriarchy, neuro-homogeneity (what used to be called sanity, and rightly so), ableism, fat phobia, etc., in a surge of what one academic in the STEM field recently called the movement for "redress and revolt."[1]

But it is not the least of the intellectual and moral distortions of this era that people have convinced themselves—or been convinced of—that, to sincerely believe something is proof of that belief's truth—assuming, of course, that the belief in question is in sync with the current identitarian wisdom. In the words of Fidel Castro (who, in fairness, would have despised Woke), "Within the Revolution, everything goes; against the Revolution, nothing."[2] To put the matter starkly, now that it has become plausible to speak of 'my truth,' even when it is at odds with 'the' truth, there can be no more objective correlatives, only subjective ones. This is the reason why being offended by something is endowed not just with the ennobling aura of victimhood and martyrdom, but entirely determined by the feelings of those who feel themselves offended. The oppressed are always right, as it were; which does not, to put it charitably, align with the universal realities of our common flawed humanity. To the contrary, Fanon—one of the identitarian left's heroes—understood perfectly that the victim can easily become the victimizer and, in some cases, even yearns to be so transformed. In that sense, DEI, and identitarian politics more broadly, are wishful thinking weaponized.

ON A PODCAST CALLED "ALL-IN" that he co-hosts, the billionaire venture capitalist Chamath Palihapitiya declared,

> Nobody cares about what's happening to the Uyghurs [...] I'm telling you a very hard, ugly truth, okay, of all the things that I care about, yes, it is below my line.[1]

His remarks were met with general outrage on social media. Even the Golden State Warriors basketball team—in which Palihapitiya is an investor—was quick to distance itself from his remarks. In a press release, Warriors management was at pains to point out that Palihapitiya was a "limited investor [with] no day-to-day operating functions with the Warriors." "Mr. Palihapitiya," the statement continued, "does not speak on behalf of our franchise, and his views certainly don't reflect those of our organization."[2]

Within forty-eight hours, Palihapitiya had done a partial climbdown, admitting in an X post that his comments "lacked empathy," and insisting that he believed "that human rights matter, whether in China, the United States, or elsewhere."[3]

Left largely ignored in the general excitement was what Palihapitiya had gone on to say when he insisted that what he cared about was,

> the fact that our economy could turn on a dime if China invades Taiwan. I care about climate change. I care about America's crippling and decrepit health-care infrastructure.[4]

It was necessary to ignore this because these comments

faithfully represent the Silicon Valley consensus that is genuinely worried about climate change and about the state of the United States, but who don't fear a Chinese invasion of Taiwan not because Taiwan is a democracy and China is a tyranny, but because they know it will be a catastrophe for their businesses, international trade, and the stock markets.

Even with regard to the Uyghurs, Palihapitiya's views were hardly as unrepresentative as people pretended. He was wrong to say that nobody in America cares what is happening to the Uyghurs. People do care, in the sense that when they see reports about what is going on they are appalled. But had Palihapitiya said that while Americans care, they don't care *that much*, he would have been on solid ground. It is not just that US corporations have no intention of stopping their business with China because of the Uyghurs; it is that some activists and people of conscience aside—and if one is being truthful, they are a small minority—Americans are not boycotting Chinese goods (mind, they are so ubiquitous that it would be almost impossible to do so affordably). Nor are college campuses riven by demands that the endowments divest from companies that trade with China, as there is with regard to fossil fuel companies and the State of Israel.

What Palihapitiya had actually done was to foolishly say publicly what practically the entire business establishment and, if we are being honest, most Americans think privately. Just as, despite the DC policy establishment's best efforts, there is no support to going to war with Russia over Ukraine, there is also no significant support for provoking a trade crisis with China over the Uyghurs. But social media is an indignation machine, a sanctimony factory, and one is simply not supposed to voice such things.

A startling detail in this mass exercise in self-flattery and self-absolution the piling on Palihapitiya's statement has been is that even with regard to what may very well be a genocide, much of the reaction on X has been expressed in terms of hurt feelings. An example was a Tweet by the human rights lawyer Rayhan Asat, who excoriated Palihapitiya for failing "to even acknowledge how his comment was hurtful to the Uyghur community," and also how his statement had provided "comfort" to China. It is not that Asat's comments were wrong, so much as how depoliticized and, indeed, depoliticizing they were.

But the distinction between the personal and the political has been lost now, just as the distinction between metaphor and reality had been lost. Ours is an era rendered mindless by its refusal to acknowledge any real difference of serious consequence between the metaphorical and the real. That this is a prophylactic against thought should be obvious. But it is also a prophylactic against serious action. Of course, everyone knows this somewhere, which is why virtue signaling—as much, if not more, to oneself as to others—has become the signature gesture of the age, an age of bad faith in which the performative guilt of today's professional managerial class bears the same relationship to real shame and real guilt as Astro Turf does to grass.

V-DEM IS A SWEDISH THINK TANK, based in the political science department of the University of Gothenburg. Founded in 2014, it has since issued annually what it called a 'Democracy Report.' In some ways, these reports resemble those issued by Freedom House, but the differences in how the two institutions describe and situate their findings are considerable. Freedom House is straightforwardly a policy shop, principally seeking to influence the US government. As the institution's website puts it:

> Freedom House advocates for U.S. leadership and collaboration with like-minded governments to vigorously oppose dictators and oppression, and strengthen democracy around the world.[1]

In other words, it espouses the views of the liberal policy establishment in Washington, which can be summarized as being that, for all its faults, a US-led international order is preferable to all other alternatives on offer, and must be maintained starting with undoing the damage Donald Trump is assumed to have done to it.

In contrast, V-Dem's house style is cooly analytic. On its website, it portrays itself as being "one of the largest-ever social science data collection efforts with a database containing over 16 million data points." But it is also frank about its own ideological bent, pointing in particular to its Case for Democracy initiative, which was started with a grant from the European Commission, as,

> [collating] state-of-the-art research on the benefits of

democracy for economic and human development, health and socio-economic protections, environmental protection and climate action, as well as international and domestic security.[2]

I should say here, first, that I am sceptical of institutions that seek to foster and proselytize for an ideology, and, second, that the fact that liberalism (in the American sense of the term) is perhaps the first secular ideology in the history of the world not to fully acknowledge that it *is* an ideology (the human rightist subset of this is particularly florid), makes me even more sceptical of them. Nonetheless, strip the polemical character out of what both V-Dem and Freedom House are reporting, and it becomes apparent that for the past few years there are increasingly more regimes across the world that one needs sophisticated measuring tools to call 'autocratic' rather than 'democratic.'

Like many other assumptions of the immediate post-Cold War period, the view that the world was going to become increasingly democratic in the serious and enduring—rather than the purely electoral—sense was always a heady mix of NATO and, above all, of American triumphalism, wishful thinking, and liberal provincialism. Above all, it was a progress narrative that conflated the end of the Soviet empire with the end of history. Both Freedom House and the V-Dem emphasize how much global resistance there is to the autocratic tsunami sweeping the world, and are certainly empirically justified, at least to some extent, in doing so (think Tunisia, and, of course, the incredibly courageous young of Myanmar). The data they adduce does not offer much reason for optimism. In global terms, contra the expectations of the 1990s, it is autocracy, not democracy, that is becoming the rising norm.

According to the 2023 V-Dem report, "Electoral autocracies continue to be the most common regime type."[3] It cites India as having, under the Modi government, turned form the world's largest democracy into an electoral autocracy. These electoral autocracies join the long list of what the report calls 'closed autocracies.' Taken together, these two versions of autocracy are home to 68% of the world's population, while full liberal democracies diminished from forty-one countries in 2010 to thirty-two in 2020, with a population share of only 14%. Electoral, but not fully liberal, democracies account for sixty nations and the remaining 19% of the population.

Reading the V-Dem study, one wonders why was any optimism about the democratization of the world ever so powerful in the first place. For, as the report points out, while the number of liberal democracies increased from twenty in 1972 and peaking at forty-one in 2010, "[t]he uptake in the number of countries over [these] years was not matched by increasing shares of the population of the world." The news during this period, the report insists, was actually much better than that. "At its peak in 1999," the report goes on, "72 countries with about 30% of the global population were in a process of democratization."

That trend has now been reversed in what V-Dem calls "the third wave of autocratization." By 2020, the same report says, "more than one-third (34%) of the world's population were living in countries undergoing autocratization while a miniscule 4% were living in democratizing nations." And, in all, V-Dem calculated that by 2020, eighty-seven states, comprising 68% of the world's population, live in some form of autocracy, up from 48% in 2010.

To be sure, as the writer Samuel Moyn said of the arguments of Steven Pinker, "a data dump is not a philosophy of history."[4] Obviously, the pattern of the previous decade could be reversed in this one. And since hope is a (non-falsifiable) metaphysical category, one can do just that: hope, if one is inclined, that things begin again to start going liberal democracy's way. But optimism is an empirical category, and there is no particular empirical basis for thinking this. The vastly increased power that the state acquired during the pandemic is not likely to be discarded afterwards—at least in most countries. Meanwhile, the process of the continued *relative* decline of the Euro-American world as compared to Northeast Asia (economic for now but, if this follows the historical pattern, soon to be cultural and intellectual as well) is likely to continue and perhaps—though this is far less sure—accelerate.

My own view is that, in the future, the term 'democracy' itself will become unstable. After all, the BJP Hindu nationalist government in India considers itself to be democratic because it is majoritarian. And the People's *Republic* of China has never conceded that it is undemocratic. And now, the Chinese State uses the language of anti-imperialism to deny its own autocratic character. For example, the Chinese foreign minister, Wang Yi, recently said tartly that, "Democracy is not Coca-Cola, which, with syrup produced in the United States, tastes the same across the world." He might as well have been channeling his inner Ariel Dorfman or Eduardo Galeano! And he met the 'autocratic accusation' head-on. It was wrong to describe China as 'authoritarian,' he said. China was a democracy, he insisted; it was just that China's democracy "takes a different form than that of the United States."[5]

This is a line that is hardly exclusive to Chinese officialdom. In an online zine called *Rest of the World* which bills itself as "reporting global tech stories,"[6] a recent piece profiles Andy Tian, who is a veteran of both the US and Chinese tech world. Tian worked for Google and then struck out on his own in a series of ventures, culminating in his current one: a Beijing-based company called Asia Innovations Group (AIG). The company is mainly an app developer focused on its live-streaming platform, Up-Live. The app makes money not from its broadcasters (that is, those who live-stream on it) but from their fans and followers, who are encouraged to give them virtual gifts, a percent of the cost of each one of them pocketed by Up-Live.[7]

In a recent interview, Tian offered his own version of Wang Yi's argument about democracy taking a different form in China than it had in the United States: The 'first stage' of tech innovation had been in the US, Tian insisted. But Chinese entrepreneurs such as himself were going to change all that. "What's the next stage of [tech] evolution?" he asked rhetorically. And proceeded to answer his own question. "[Those of us] based in emerging markets," Tian boasted, "we are taking over." And then he concluded with a flourish. "We are decolonizing," he said.[8]

Autocracy and Woke. A marriage made in heaven.

And more likely to end in lifelong harmony than in eventual divorce. Wisecracks aside, the liberal democratic order was always going to end, as all political systems end, just as surely as individual human lives do. The only important question was *when* it would end. Everything I see around me, read, watch, suggests that the answer is that it will be sooner rather than later—that is, if it is not ending already.

THE NOVELIST AND CRITIC Ryan Ruby wrote on X that,

> what is historically unique about today's ultra-rich, as a class, is that they show no interest in high culture, least of all literature. Things have gotten so bad that taste is no longer required to legitimate wealth or to distinguish the ultra-rich from potential competitors.[1]

This sense that, today, being a patron of high culture is no longer needed, and, indeed, may actually create an obstacle to the social legitimation that individual Maecenases and corporate sponsors have heretofore sought to obtain through cultural benefactions, explains the abandonment (and sometimes even the repudiation) of high culture by the donor class far more convincingly than the conspiracy theories on the right about the kidnapping of culture by Woke and Critical Race Theory and all that, or than the triumphalism of the cultural bureaucrats of the new cultural dispensation who believe themselves to have wrested the commanding heights of the culture from the old elite and are at last opening it up to the excluded and the marginalized. In reality, 'social justice' cultural critique was pushing on an open door. For this, too, Ryan Ruby offers an illuminating explanation. For the ultra-rich, he writes,

> depth and refinement are a liability, since the maintenance of their class position relies on state capture, which in turn requires not alienating too many people.[2]

There is a parallel to be drawn here with the

transformation of the dress codes of male aristocrats of Europe at the beginning of the nineteenth century. Before that, magnificence was the hallmark of male aristocratic dress (and, with the rise of the bourgeoisie, of those who wanted to copy aristocratic habits of dress). But beginning in the Regency in England and quickly spreading across Europe, magnificence gave way to extremely sober, generally dark-hued clothing.

Of course, this too was a class marker. One had to know the codes to understand why one black coat set you apart as an aristocrat, while another identified you as a tradesman. What marked you sartorially as an aristocratic male went from being exoteric—that is, with silks, furs, jewels, and the rest, obvious to all—to being esoteric—that is, visible only to those in on the secret. Today, of course, the reverse is the case in that the rich dress ever more informally, as if any hint of magnificence would—following Ruby's argument—alienate people too much. An extreme version of this is found in the tech world, where T-shirts and trainers are practically the uniform (though shorts *à la* Sam Bankman-Fried mercifully remain a rarity, for now anyway) of billionaires. But the increasing tendency of Wall Street financiers to go tieless, itself an emblem of the general relaxation of dress codes among the rich and the high bourgeoisie (including the political class, especially in Europe, that takes its lead from them) suggests that obvious signs of dress are no longer necessary and, like an interest in high culture, off-putting to too many people.

Obviously, there are other sources of this informality, notably as a manifestation of the culture-wide desire of adults not to be adults, which understandably makes dressing like an adolescent hard to resist. Bling will never die, of course, but, if anything, the ultra-rich as a caste seem less interested in bling than, say, footballers, pop singers, and high-end criminal lawyers. In New York it can sometimes seem as if the only men who dress as grownups did fifty years ago are Black ministers and homicide detectives. But I think Ruby's intuition is the deeper one: state capture requires not standing out in a crowd, lest the punters take fright.

Where does this leave culture? To be sure, cultural production where there is serious money involved—above all painting and architecture—still command the attention of the ultra-rich. But while cultural production with no financial value—above all, as Ruby rightly notes, literature, but to which one might add theater and classical music—still needs money, this money comes not from the ultra-rich directly but through foundations established with the money of previous generations of the ultra-rich. The people who run these philanthropies do not need to distinguish themselves from potential competitors, for they have none, save for the state itself. Instead, the need to define themselves as moral arbiters, which makes funding art and literature with a social purpose far more attractive than with writing, painting, and sculpture that confers no easier access to the moral high ground, and may even block entry to it entirely.

High culture is difficult, demanding, and often off-putting. It requires single-minded focus in a world where single-minded focus is, along with silence, the rarest of commodities. In contrast, popular culture is easy on the neurons, while popular culture that is also presented as being an artifact of and a conduit toward social justice and inclusion is easy on the conscience as well. That this is a kitsch version of conscience—in Milan Kundera's sense of one thinking better of oneself for having consumed it, a form of virtue-signaling whether in the context of enjoyment, atonement, or both—not only is no longer troubling to most people, it is no longer even visible to them. In an era where dissent is commodified, and the young are informed by a particularly extreme form of subjective idealism, and apocalypse is very much *l'air du temps*, it could hardly be otherwise. What makes Woke so appealing to so many is that it is apocalyptic but not pessimistic. Call it the banality of antinomianism.

THE WOKE VISION of culture is no different from its vision of society: the only morally licit culture is a representative one, with representation defined largely in demographic and/or sociological terms, but emphatically not in terms of class. A recent example of this is *The New York Times*' recent announcement that it was creating a series of fellowships to diversify the ranks of the people who create crosswords. The announcement specified that the goal of these fellowships was intended "to provide mentorship and support for constructors from underrepresented groups, including women, people of color and the L.G.B.T.Q. community." The announcement went on to say that the *Times* wants its puzzles to "reflect the reality of all Americans, which means we want to publish work that reflects a diverse range of cultural reference points, language usage and communities."[1]

But even if one accepts one of the basic premises of Woke and of Kendi/DiAngelo-style CRT (which now dominate much of the academe and the publishing world and virtually all of the cultural-philanthropic complex, which is that culture is representation and representation is culture) the absence of class is striking and offers one more example (as if another were needed!) of Adolph Reed, Jr.'s quip that the real project of Woke was to diversify the ruling class. But DEI provides a simulacrum of justice, and that is more than good enough. For, in an age of virtue-signaling, if the wishful thinking is not supported by the facts, then so much the worse for the facts.

IT SHOULD, BY NOW, be obvious to everyone but the most purblind followers of Woke and Kendi/DiAngelo-style 'anti-racism' that the ghost at the banquet of their millenarian hopes is the ghost of class. There are a number of reasons for this—some obvious and some less so. But at its core, the explanation is quite simple: it is not only possible to be an anti-racist *à la* Kendi/DiAngelo without having any idea or, for that matter, any ambition to change the economic system—it is almost a requirement. In this sense, the Woke and the anti-racists of today are all performing variations on the theme of José Vasconcelos's famous admonition, "For my people, the spirit will speak."[1] For, once class becomes a central part of the equation, the demand for 'representation' no longer remains so clear-cut, the question of for whom one's spirit is speaking no longer so self-evident.

But assume, for the sake of argument, that the Kendi/DiAngelo formula were to become the norm, and in the professional managerial classes every identity were to come to be represented along fairly rigid demographic lines: whites are *w* percent of the population, blacks are *x*, women are *y*, trans are *z*, and so on. This should not be difficult to envisage, given the fact that, to a considerable extent, this effort is quite far advanced in the academic-cultural-philanthropic complex. Assume, further, that libraries, concert halls, book publishing, etc. were 'retrofitted' to conform to what, for lack of a better term, I'll call these 'duties of equitable representation.' The result would indeed be transformative, but it would leave the economic structures of society utterly untouched.

One of the principal reasons for this, is that, what the Woke and their sympathizers refer to as "a moment of racial reckoning in the West" is, precisely, not a moment of *class* reckoning. If anything, it is its opposite. One could utterly transform the racial, gender, and sexual preference profile of any institution without even touching its class character. Indeed, that is precisely what is being done at present, and why, as I have argued elsewhere, the corporate mainstreaming of Woke has been so easily set in motion. Robin DiAngelo in her books talks *ad nauseam* about the shame she feels about her white privilege. But to the extent she talks about class at all, it is as its being one of the rewards of White Supremacy, which in an era when certain non-white immigrant groups in the United States now have higher income levels, better educational and health outcomes, etc. than whites, clearly is, to be charitable, an incomplete picture. Without class accounted for, the Woke paradigm is like an alphabet with no vowels.

BY NOW, TO OBSERVE that modern progressive thought is focused on the specificities of race and gender while being largely indifferent to the commonalities of class has become commonplace. Du Bois's famous aphorism that "the problem of the twentieth century is the problem of the color line" is assumed to apply just as comprehensively to the twenty-first. The apparent problem with this argument—as even its advocates sometimes uneasily acknowledge—is that, while it is possible to argue that during the centuries of Europe's global hegemony, and latterly that of the United States, one could insist on the inseparability of racism and capitalism, the rise of Northeast Asia—first of Japan and South Korea, but above all now of China—would seem to sunder that theory of inseparability. Surely, one cannot simultaneously insist that the United States is in inexorable relative decline, and that at the very least we are entering an era of both political and capitalist multipolarity (if not one of outright Chinese pre-eminence within the capitalist global system) and also insist that capitalism and White Supremacy are inseparable. And, yet, that is precisely what modern progressives do, and they have succeeded to the point that their view has now become the consensus within the academic-cultural-philanthropic complex and, increasingly within the professional managerial class as a whole.

One might have thought that the fact that neither the Chinese, nor the South Koreans, nor the Japanese are white might have sown at least a measure of doubt into the verdant acreage of this consensus. But, instead, those who insist that capitalism and racism are inseparable have remained undaunted.

To the contrary, the well-known Australian political journalist and academic Stan Grant wrote recently that "too often the conversation around the rise of [China as this] new superpower is in predominantly geo-political terms."[1] In reality, Grant argues, it is "race [that] sits at the heart of it all." If in the West, China is seen as a threat to the "so-called global rules-based order," that is because that order itself is "routed in a race-based order."

I am by no means certain that the case for White Supremacy and capitalism having been historically inseparable is as strong as its partisans make out. What I am sure about is that it is a poor moral, economic, and political template for understanding capitalism's present, let alone its future. Grant insists that "race and racism inform China's rise" and claims that Mao Tse-tung "styled himself as the revolutionary leader of the non-white world." Again, even assuming for the sake of argument that Grant is right, the relevant fact is that, despite the continuity of the absolute hegemony of the Chinese Communist Party, Maoist China was anti-capitalist while Xi's China is capitalist. Indeed, there are some who believe that the Chinese version of capitalism is proving itself superior to the Euro-American one. To borrow an image of Leonard Cohen's, the reality is that in 2022 White Supremacy increasingly looks like a shining artifact of [capitalism's] past.

But Grant and the many others who share his view across the Anglosphere cannot let go of the concept of Whiteness as the root of all that is wrong with the world. So how to keep afloat the doctrine of capitalism in any form, and White Supremacy being indivisible and permanent? The only solution is the one Grant comes up with: he turns Whiteness into a synonym for power, even if the people wielding that power are not white themselves. The Chinese Communist Party, he writes, including under Xi, "has a deep racial consciousness." And this consciousness is focused on the century-long radicalized humiliation "at the hands of foreign powers—of white powers." But here Grant has to acknowledge that "this humiliation was also at the hands of the Japanese." But this does not give him pause. "The Japanese themselves," he writes, "cannot be separated from the project of whiteness." Yes, it too was imperial, but "its imperialism mirrored the imperialism of white colonizers."

That, if anything, Japan wanted to overthrow white colonizers and rule in their stead, does not seem to occur to Grant. Imperialism is a White Supremacist construct and, therefore, to be an imperialist power is to be a white power, even if you are, well, non-white. And, say what you will about Grant, he carries this argument to its logical conclusion. Xi's China might have represented the end of whiteness, he laments, but instead "the Chinese Communist Party itself mirrors whiteness." How can this be? Well, it has turned out that Xi is a Han nationalist, committed to the idea that "Chinese power is ethnic Han superiority."

Grant is probably right about this. But instead of this leading him to question his own efforts to put all forms of capitalism—including the Chinese—indeed, arguably, all forms of power into the Procrustean Bed of White Supremacy, Grant doubles down, insisting that Han persecution of non-Han is nothing less white people persecuting non-white people.

One feels as if one has entered a lunatic asylum. The Han are not white, and somehow they are. But in Grant's world—and in this he is in no sense expressing a fringe view but rather is an emblematic figure of a very wide current of an opinion—whiteness is a synonym for power, period. Thus, for Grant, the tragedy of Xi's China is that it has become what he believes historically it opposed: whiteness—of which, he says, "Xi Xinping is its champion…the continuation of white power in darker skin."

Whiteness as metaphor, in short. It is this metaphorization of understanding that is the deepest intellectual, and in some ways, the deepest philosophical ill that afflicts us because it leads the culture toward a refusal to acknowledge any difference between the metaphorical and the real.

NARCISSISM AND PROVINCIALITY in the service of virtue remain narcissism and provinciality. This, rather than the specific political views of those concerned, is the deep problem with the hegemonic ideological role that Woke plays in education in the US and in Canada (and to some extent in Australia and New Zealand). For, the principal subject goes from being what is being studied to who is doing the studying. Once you make education a largely moral and political project, you have, in effect, established a kind of Procrustean Bed onto which the subject matter itself must be made to fit.

The challenge in the US to elite schools that heretofore granted admission almost entirely on the basis of competitive examinations is a prime example of this. The argument is quite straightforward: the student bodies of these schools have never reflected the ethnic or racial make-up of the communities in which they are situated. Therefore, there must be something fundamentally wrong with the admissions process.

The rhetoric that has often accompanied these claims involves misrepresentations of demographic reality that would be comic, were they not so damaging. The foremost of these is that these elite schools are bastions of White Supremacy. And, yet, the reality is that if this was ever so these schools are bastions of Asian-American endeavor, to the point that Asian-American students are almost everywhere the majority in urban elite schools and often in suburban ones too.

But if what you expect of schooling is the furtherance of the Woke and Kendi/DiAngelo style 'anti-racism' project—that is, if what is central is the moral imperative of achieving Diversity, Equity, and Inclusion (DEI)—

then what schools have traditionally been expected to do (teach people things they don't already know) may still be important but can no longer be considered the first priority.

To be sure, this is not the way the project is described by its proselytizers. Instead, they come up with increasingly inventive ways of concealing the fact that what they are calling for is demographic representation to be considered more important than keeping the standards embodied in test scores. 'Inclusive excellence' is the operative euphemism.

And yet, of course, excellence is rarely inclusive. That's why it's called 'excellence.' But this is precisely what is being challenged today. And to do this successfully, you have to change the nature of schooling, and move it from teaching young subjects to affirming (another euphemism: what is meant is 'celebrating') their identities and experiences—that is to say, therapeutizing, as well as politicizing, learning. And, so, in yet another way, the post-Protestant celebration of the self becomes paramount.

Education is now a morality play in which the fact that subjects like mathematics or physics are actually very hard is occluded, and the ethical project in which, indeed, everyone is qualified to join becomes paramount. In this vision of things, to do anything else is to exclude, to marginalize, to reject; in short, to uphold injustice.

In the name of ethics, ethical complexity is being lost. In the name of representation, talent becomes an instrument of oppression; unless, that is, everyone is held up as being talented, which, again, is a contradiction in terms. But that is now the orthodox view.

> The crisis consists precisely in the fact that the old is dying and the new cannot be born; in this interregnum a great variety of morbid symptoms appear. — Gramsci[1]

> If we want things to stay as they are, things will have to change — Lampedusa[2]

THESE TWO FAMOUS QUOTATIONS from the great Marxist thinker and from the great Italian novelist encapsulate two very different ways critics of Woke and of Kendi/DiAngelo 'anti-racism' look at the underlying reasons for its success. The Gramsci quote is bound to appeal to anti-Woke voices on the left. By this, I mean people who indeed believe the present order needs to be overturned, but reject Woke's moral absolutism, its disdain for class politics and for coalition-building with groups with which it will have fundamental disagreements, as—to cite a glaring example—gay women's groups unwilling to accept all the premises of trans, and its balkanization of identities accompanied by the demand that each one of these identities being represented and included. Think of what started as the LGTB rainbow flag and of how it now has so many stripes in it that it resembles the endless quarterings of aristocratic Hapsburg family crests that one can see in editions of the Almanac de Gotha.

It should be obvious that the Gramsci quote can hold little appeal for liberals. For most of them, after all, liberalism is not dying at all but, rather, it is being terribly and hatefully besieged from both its right and its left; or, if it is now at risk of being consigned to the dustbin of ideology, its wounds are self-inflicted, the product of an unwarranted crisis of confidence, a failure of nerve. Thus, it needs to stop apologizing and start reinvigorating itself, to become what it was throughout most of the Cold War, a "fighting faith," as Arthur Schlesinger, Jr. famously put it. And, even more obviously, Gramsci's apothegm can have no possible appeal to the right, despite perhaps resonating to the idea of Woke as a 'morbid symptom,' since what it is seeking is restoration, not revolution.

But for those of us, whatever else we think of it, believe that Woke—while in no sense a full-fledged ideology because of its utter failure to address either class or the economy in a serious and sustained way—offers the most powerful and compelling set of moral and cultural ideas in the West at least since the disenchantment with Communism produced first by the collapse of the USSR and then by Deng Xiaoping's transformation of China into an authoritarian capitalist state, these calls for the moral rearmament of liberalism sound like nothing so much as whistling past the ideological graveyard. For the truth is that the motley of moral and cultural ideas that make up Woke are now so influential among middle-class and particularly upper-middle-class young people, and even among many older members of the professional managerial classes that capitalism could not possibly have ignored them, if for no other reason than that these young people continue to flock to Wall Street, corporate law, and the other high-earning professions, in percentages no smaller than the non-Woke generations that preceded them, and that, even if only a cultural style, few of these young people come from arrive uninfluenced by at least a strain or two of Woke. Liberals, of course, rightly see Woke as a threat. But to assume that corporations should take the same view is arrant wishful thinking.

The liberals' confusion about this is understandable, for on university campuses, in the art galleries and museums, in the literary world, and of course in the big establishment philanthropies such as Ford and Mellon, the ambient political and cultural noise is floridly anti-capitalist. There is talk of capitalism being inseparable from racism (Asia, as usual, being virtually never taken into account as having a capitalist history of its own, not to mention a capitalist future that is likely to be far brighter than that of the West). And, an academic in the geography department of Oxford University boasts of practicing 'disobedient scholarship' in an institution she calls "the belly of the beast"[3] (this is only one of countless iterations of such a view within academe; they vary very little in tone or underlying conviction). More broadly, from within what I have taken to calling 'the academic-cultural-philanthropic complex', both education and culture are seen as instruments of social transformation with anything falling short of those goals being a moral outrage.

Faced with this, to paraphrase *The Rolling Stones*'s "Street Fighting Man," what can a poor capitalist class do than play for a rock and roll band, aka to co-opt this radicalism? This has been done with regard to leading individuals, as when the supposedly intransigent Ta-Nehisi Coates was hired by Warner Brothers to do the screenplay for the studio's next *Superman* vehicle; or the deal—since canceled—that

Netflix struck with Ibram X. Kendi to produce a series based on Kendi's children's book, *Anti-Racist Baby*. It can be done systemically, largely through adopting Woke speech codes, most notably so-called 'inclusive' language, as most of Silicon Valley has already done, and insisting staff attend Diversity, Equity, and Inclusion workshops and retreats, which is increasingly the norm, rather than the exception, in corporate America, in Canada, and in the UK.

And this co-optation has been overwhelmingly successful. The CIA's most recent recruitment ad features an agent speaking of intersectionality, and does not differ much from the Woke ads that corporations like Nike, seeking to appeal to young people, have been running for some time. Kendi may still say he's an anti-capitalist, but accepting a Netflix offer is an odd way to signal it. I am, of course, being sarcastic: on campus, Woke may still claim to be radical, and the vulgarized and distorted (read Kendi-ite) version of Critical Race Theory that is common intellectual currency there may still prevail (we are a long way from Randall Kennedy's CRT, as he himself has frequently pointed out). But in the outside world, these supposedly 'disobedient' ideas, to quote my Oxford geographer, are being ever so gently but also inexorably disciplined.

People on the right see this, of course, and they speak bitterly of Woke Capitalism, and of their determination to defeat it. But what they have not understood is that taming Woke is a far more important task for the corporations, for whom this new generation of the professional managerial class is rightly viewed as corporate America's future. Could corporations 'lay down the law,' as conservative activists keep demanding? Perhaps. But why should they? Adapting to changing times, rewriting the rules of the game, in a storm bending like a willow rather than cracking like an oak: this is what capitalism does best. In an age of racism, it was racist; in an age of Woke, it will be Woke. So long, that is, as the bottom line is not affected. And it has not been affected. This is why the Lampedusa quote offers a far more convincing description of the current moment than Gramsci's. "If we want things to stay as they are, things will have to change" says Prince Tancredi, the principal figure in Lampedusa's masterpiece, *The Leopard*. And that is exactly what is happening now.

FOR CAPITALISM, the politics of atonement—which, when all is said and done, is what identitarian progressivism is all about—has turned out to be a little more than a post-modern version of the indulgences sold by the Medieval Church, an essential moral emollient for a fundamentally ruthless, grasping, and immoral neoliberal academy (and, by extension, its dependencies in culture and its sponsors in the philanthropies) as the sale of indulgences was for a ruthless, grasping, and fundamentally immoral medieval Catholic Church. That is why those who call DEI bureaucrats 'grifters' have got it wrong. For, to call someone 'a grifter' implies that they are committing some form of fraud, and there is no fraud going on in this context. To the contrary, the DEI ideology performs the essential service of conferring moral legitimacy on a Western capitalist system that, with the decline of Christianity and the hollowing out of the nation state, was sorely in need of it. To change historical analogies, Woke is the Potemkin Village, the neoliberal university the Stalinist reality. This is why, in our era, neoliberalism cannot do without Woke.

Exhibit A

The American Medical Association recently issued a document called "Advancing Health Equity: A Guide to Language, Narrative and Concepts." At first glance, one could be forgiven for thinking that it was written by revolutionary graduate students in some university English department. "We are continually called," it intones, quasi-religiously (as does so much Woke and anti-racism Ibram X. Kendi/Robin DiAngelo-style rhetoric), "to be better as we lead this work toward the pursuit of racial justice, equity and liberation."[1]

One would never know that, for the AMA, this liberation absolutely excludes major reform of the hospital payment system which daily ruins countless American families or, indeed, *any* reform that risks hitting its members in their pocketbooks.

Exhibit B

The Kaiser Permanente Health System, which is the largest managed care organization in the United States, with over 300,000 employees, recently organized Kendi-inflected anti-racism sessions for their California employees titled, "Providing Culturally and Linguistically Appropriate Services in California." Some of it is Woke/Kendi/DiAngelo boilerplate, though there is a curious passage in which participants are warned of unconscious bias and stereotyping that might make them HIRE Asian-Americans in finance departments of the organization because of stereotyped thinking that leads them to assume Asian-Americans are good at math. Left unaddressed is the question of whether this means that Asian-American candidates should therefore be turned away, or graded more severely, thus limiting their access to these jobs (much as happens routinely, though largely informally, to Asian-Americans applying to Ivy League universities).

One would never know that Kaiser forces everybody who signs up for one of its health plans to accept that, in the event of a dispute between the plan holder and the company, the plan holder will have no right to go to court to seek redress but must, instead, accept binding (private) arbitration, over which Kaiser has already pre-set the ground rules. As for Kaiser's employees, well, recently the Kaiser Permanente Antioch Medical Center gave its nurses "'An Encouragement Stone' as a thank you for Nurses week." "Keep the rock or give it to a friend," the leaflet accompanying this 'gift' to the nursing staff enjoins, "as a reminder that the work you do ROCKS!"[2] [Capitalized in the original.]

Whether Woke ever was the emancipatory doctrine so many of its adherents on university campuses have been proclaiming it to be is still an open question. What is clear, though, is that it is no longer one but, instead, is now central to what one of Woke's severest critics, Adolph Reed, Jr.—like so many of Woke's most determined adversaries, himself a person of the hard left—has called the project of "diversifying the ruling class."[3] One might add that, in an era where liberalism seems totally exhausted (my view is that it is unsalvageable but, then, I'm not a liberal), an era of anxiety and generalized moral and material panic, above all over climate change, Woke, Kendi, DiAngelo are all increasingly providing moral bona fides for the status quo. That, it seems to me, and not some failure of will that the American right keeps pointing to, is the key to the movement's success. In short, emancipatory nominalism and pet rocks: a perfect couple for the early twenty-first century.

BRECHT'S FAMOUS PRESCRIPTION, "First grub, then ethics," would simply not fly in today's academic-cultural-philanthropic complex. Yes, there too the rhetoric is often anti-capitalist, but it is based on a praxis diametrically opposed to Brecht's: "First ethics, then grub." Hence the pathological nihilism where more energy is devoted to renaming buildings on campuses and removing public monuments than to advocating for small business loans, better mass transit, or the expansion of health care. To be clear, I'm not saying that the Woke don't care about these material questions but, rather, that they don't expend one-tenth the energy on them that they do on symbolic politics.

And those symbolic politics are a mixed bag even in their own terms. The removing of the statues commemorating the Confederacy seems to me to have been an entirely good thing, even if I think the Woke iconoclasts have now taken to making demands that will do more harm than good, such as calling for the removal of statues of Washington and of Lincoln. On the other hand, so-called 'Land Acknowledgment,' where before a public event, the organizers and speakers *acknowledge* that the event is taking place on land settlers stolen from indigenous people, borders on the ridiculous. This is not because the story of dispossession is not true—it obviously is—but because the people making these 'acknowledgments' have not the slightest intention of giving the land back to its original inhabitants. In the culture industry (the Brooklyn Academy of Music (BAM) in New York City, where I live, exemplifies this) land acknowledgments have become the norm, but this does not mean these same cultural and academic institutions don't continue to try to raise vast sums of money for construction and other capital improvements. One awaits the moment—surely it can't be long now!— when realtors selling properties in urban neighbourhoods where a Woke cultural consensus prevails will themselves begin their sales pitches with land acknowledgments. A nice co-op apartment plus a bit of moral expiation first: what could more perfectly sum up the cultural and material habits of the professional managerial classes of era, at least in the US, Canada, the UK, and Australia (and increasingly in Chile and Argentina too)?

Indeed, even claiming that in the current cultural and moral climate the Brecht quotation has been flipped on its head to put ethics first and grub second may be overgenerous. "First ethics, then more ethics," or even "Ethics *is* grub," is likely closer to the mark.

WALTER BENJAMIN FAMOUSLY SAID that every document of civilization is also a document of barbarism. This is, I think, a statement of fact, not an interpretation—though we might add that it is rare for societies to keep both aspects of Benjamin's idea in their collective consciousness at the same time. Rather, societies tend to oscillate between focusing on the civilization and focusing on the barbarism. That is certainly what has happened in the Anglosphere and in parts of Latin America (I cannot speak confidently of other regions), and happened seemingly in the blinking of an eye. But then, as the saying goes, "There are decades where nothing happens; and there are weeks where decades happen." The popular unrest that roiled the US in the summer following the murder of George Floyd—the term 'insurrection' still seems to me excessive, but there were certainly elements of insurrection in what took place—was a case of exactly those rare weeks Lenin was evoking. Ideas that theretofore had seemed comparatively weak suddenly seemed powerful, not to say *irresistible*, while the established order, at least the symbolic order as represented by language, by monuments, by festivals (Thanksgiving and Columbus Day in the US, for example), and the rest seemed past their moral and ideological sell-by dates.

It seems simply unimaginable, to cite two Latin American examples, that the statues of the Spanish conquistadors who conquered Chile and were torn down during the so-called 'social explosion' (*estallido social*) that wracked the country between October 2019 and March 2020 will ever be restored to their plinths, anymore than the replacing of the statue of Columbus in the heart of Mexico City by a statue to an indigenous woman will ever be reversed. That these radical 'rewritings' of Chile's, or Mexico's, or the United States' pasts lay waste to the established symbolic order but leave the economic order unscathed—in some cases even strengthened, as I would argue the adoption by corporate America of a mainstreamed Woke has been—is a separate issue, albeit a crucial one in the broader context of where capitalism is heading.

But while we most emphatically do *not* stand at the threshold of an era in which the last really shall be first and the first last (to the contrary, the first have never had it so good), the artifacts of the Western past that were long presented as exemplifying civilization at its highest are now increasingly seen as glorifying barbarism at its lowest. That, presumably, was what Arthur Miller had in mind when he wrote that, "An era can be said to end when its basic illusions have been exhausted,"[1] and that seems to be the point we have reached. Like an airplane during take-off, there is a certain point when it has reached a speed at which it is impossible to abort. The problem is that the 'successor illusions' seem incredibly thin. For some reason, I am drawn to quotes from Lenin again: "Communism is Soviet power plus the electrification of the whole country."[2] The problem with Woke and 'anti-racism' is that while it has lots of ideas about power, it doesn't have the first clue about electrification. And its utopian folly is to somehow believe this does not matter.

I DOUBT VERY MUCH THAT the goal of those who have championed, and largely succeeded in, making normative the Identitarian/Woke/Critical Race Theory transformation of the academic-cultural-philanthropic complex was to deprive the countries of the Global North and, above all, the Anglosphere, of the capacity to retain antibodies to the total dominion of consumer capitalism. But, whatever the original purpose, this is likely to be the deepest and most long-lasting effect of the transformation. Right-wing critics have called 'Woke-ized,' identitarian, education a system for what one French critic called the manufacture of cretins. But, while the popular culture that, in the name of equity, is the nail with which the identitarians require to dispatch high culture once and for all (only putting Western Civilization in its current debased form out of its misery can clear the way for a new high culture—one that I am virtually certain will be created in Northeast Asia and in India), what actually is being manufactured are not cretins but, rather, new generations whose hallmark psychically is an irate fragility, and whose equilibrium depends on the bureaucracies—above all in health, in education, and in culture—that ensure this fragility is simultaneously nurtured and disciplined. Ours is an age in which people routinely, even ritualistically, speak of feeling unsafe when in fact what they are is offended, and of both their psychological and physical health literally being put at risk if exposed to anything disturbing, even in a book or a film, when in fact what they are is being made uncomfortable. This is why Woke is, at its core, an expression of moral and social hypochondria.

TO DISMISS WOKE AS MERE hucksterism is too easy. Are there Woke hucksters? Of course: the names of the usual suspects come to mind virtually unbidden. But outrage over Woke, and frustration over its success, is a poor guide to understanding it. Every movement has its hucksters, and I am anything but persuaded that Woke has more than others. Far more interesting are Woke's own delusions. For, the Woke sincerely and passionately believe themselves to be redeeming culture, the humanities, and, increasingly the STEM fields as well, both ethically and intellectually. What all this blinds them to is that, in reality, they are the humanities' death rattle. This is not because, as many Woke critics are pleased to imagine, Woke are the humanities' executioners. Rather, it is because in a world where universities have either become, or are becoming, trade schools, and where the past is considered only of interest insofar as it is relevant to the present, Woke plays an extremely important role—though in fairness, largely an unwitting one—in providing the ethical grease to ease this transition.

It is the idealization of relevance that is behind the idea that the most important thing art and culture have to offer is to equitably represent communities, rather than inspire something that transcends both communities and individuals. In practical terms, within the subsidized world of the academic-philanthropic-cultural complex, this explains why *relevance* is more prized over *excellence* on moral and ethical grounds. A representative statement of this view came from the Arts Council England's deputy Chief Executive for Arts and Culture, Simon Mellor: "Relevance, not excellence, will be the new litmus test for funding."[1] It its a view seconded by the Arts Council Director of Music, Claire Mera-Nelson, who insisted that, "It is sometimes more important to think about audience opportunity than it is to always prioritize the quality of the platform."[2]

The problem here is not that what has mass appeal is always junk, whereas what appeals only to the few is always good. To say this would be mere snobbery, and too much of the critique of Woke is just that: snobbery. But what is true is that understanding certain kinds of art, just like engaging with certain forms of spiritual practice—Zen meditation is an obvious example here—and, of course, attaining athletic excellence, are very difficult things to do, and take a great deal of time, effort, and commitment. There is an old Buddhist joke about the student who goes to the Roshi and says, "Master, how long until I find enlightenment?" The master thinks, and then replies, "Ten years." Aghast, the pupils cries out, "Ten years??" To which the Roshi answers, "Twenty years."

In an important sense, the tragedy of Woke for this dying civilization is that it offers commercial culture the moral legitimation of its own mediocrity. Self-evidently, audiences with no experience of or grounding in Baroque opera, or the Bunraku, or the classical Sanskrit playwrights are going to have great difficulty appreciating it, whereas pop music or poetry jams are completely accessible immediately. The problem is that these popular forms need no subsidy, whereas higher culture does—just as they always have, whether in Tang China or Medici Florence—if they are to survive at all. But commercial culture sees no sense in keeping them alive and now, with Woke, it can justify its indifference in the name of diversity, equity, and inclusion.

The problem for the Woke, at least within the academe—but probably within the broader culture as well—is that by enforcing their Pride's Purge of Western culture, they are in effect signing their own death warrant as well. All one has to do to understand this is to look at the decline of the study of the arts and humanities in US, Canadian, and British universities. Not only are departments in many universities shutting down, but most of those that are—at least for now—surviving, including in elite universities, are doing so only by ruthlessly exploiting junior staff, most of whom now resemble itinerant sixteenth century artisans living hand to mouth with no guild to protect them. That, of course, is why so many young untenured teachers and teaching assistants are trying to escape the role universities impose on them as a kind of lumpen professoriate, and are trying to unionize.

One can only wish them luck. But at least in the arts and the humanities, it is by now a foregone conclusion that, within a decade, the struggle in university departments will not be to remake them under the sign of Woke, but for their very survival. The Woke, though, have their eyes fixed on a radiant future. They think commercial culture is their friend, when in fact it is their executioner. In their confusion, they are like the frog in the old joke about the frog and the scorpion. A frog and a scorpion meet at a stream and the scorpion asks the frog to carry him across. At first the frog refuses. "You'll sting me and I'll die," he says. But the scorpion reassures him, saying, "But I won't sting you. How could I? If I did, we would both drown." Reassured, the frog agrees. The scorpion climbs up onto his back, and they set off across the stream. Halfway across, the scorpion does sting the frog. And as they are both drowning, the frog cries out, "But why?" To which the scorpion replies, "Because I'm a scorpion."

Probably sooner rather than later, the Woke will discover that they are that frog and commercial culture is that scorpion—except that this is a scorpion that knows perfectly well how to swim.

ONE OF THE MOST STRIKING things about Robin DiAngelo's new book, *Nice Racism: How Progressive White People Perpetuate Racial Harm*, is the extent to which it is a self-help book in the grand American tradition. In Alcoholics Anonymous, for example, there something called a Twelfth Step Call, which is defined as visiting an alcoholic who has asked for help and talking about the AA program with him or with her. Further, AA sponsors have the ongoing responsibility to help a newcomer adjust to a way life without alcohol. DiAngelo's version of this is "an accountability partner," whom she defines as "a person of color with whom you have built a trusting relationship and who has agreed to coach you, talk through challenges with you, think with you and challenge you on issues of racism."[1] There are differences, obviously: DiAngelo's accountability partner is a person of color, not a reformed white racist, but AA and Kendi/DiAngelo-style 'anti-racism' share a fundamental idea, which is that the afflicted person (whether the affliction is alcoholism or White Supremacy) needs a coach to help them in their journey toward the promised lands of sobriety, or that of anti-racism that they are striving to reach.

Americans have always believed in self-transformation as something within reach of anyone who is committed enough and can find the strength to achieve it. But Americans have also tended to believe that they need coaches, whether physical or spiritual, to facilitate this transformation, and structured environments—workshops, group therapy sessions, personal trainers, etc.—where the work is to be done. The Kendi/DiAngelo recipe for how to learn to become an anti-racist and, eventually, to also learn how to become an ally of people of color, in the effort to smash White Supremacy, is entirely within the mainstream of the US self-help tradition. That, I think, is one of the most important reasons for its success—but also for the ease with which it is has come to be embraced by corporate America. DiAngelo is obsessed by her racial privileges, but not long detained by her class privileges, and that is precisely why her ideas can be mainstreamed so successfully. I doubt very much this would have been possible had she, say, used her now considerable fame and influence to support unionization efforts by Amazon workers in the United States, or the cruelties of the gig economy.

In a brilliant demolition of *Nice Racism* that he published on his blog recently, Jeffrey Aaron Snyder points to a story DiAngelo tells in the book in which she rues the fact that even she cannot maintain racial shame as long she feels she should. As an example of this she posits the following:

> Perhaps on my way into a Whole Foods I must walk past an indigenous man who appears homeless lying on the sidewalk. I see him from down the block and in that moment I become hyper-conscious of our racial positions. My whiteness suddenly feels very 'loud,' and I 'know' that he knows that I am an amnestying imposter and a hypocrite, that my privilege and comfort, my access to resources, are dependent on his position in relation to mine, dependent on his oppression.[2]

The paragraph is vulnerable to all sorts of critique, and Snyder unleashes what my late friend

Christopher Hitchens once referred to as "the full compliment of foot, horse, and gun" against DiAngelo. But what I found most interesting in the passage was the set-up: DiAngelo says that when she encountered the homeless indigenous man, she had been on her way to Whole Foods. That emporium is, to be sure, the upscale supermarket chain to end all upscale supermarket chains. I can see that DiAngelo shops there for no other reason that I shop there too. But the point about Whole Foods (which has often been referred to by its own customers as 'Whole Paycheck') is that the vast majority of Americans, very much including most white Americans, cannot afford to shop in their branches.

But while outrage—including outrage at herself, which is one of her signature moves rhetorically—clings to DiAngelo's prose like iron filings to a magnet, Whole Foods is wholly exempted from it. She doesn't even seem to see that there might be an ethical problem with that. But there, DiAngelo is in good company. After all, many of the most important, richest private schools in the United States (from Collegiate in New York, to Sidwell Friends in Washington, DC, and on to Westlake in Los Angeles) have now declared themselves to be anti-racist institutions. They are also immensely rich institutions that nonetheless charge fees so exorbitant as to be affordable by at most ten percent of American parents (and the percentage may well be quite a bit lower). Self-righteousness really doesn't get any sweeter than this.

THE PREVAILING CONFORMISM of the academic-cultural-philanthropic complex is non-conformism. Since this is a contradiction in terms—and somewhere deep down even the so-called 'non-conformists' of our day must realize this—the only way to keep the charade going is to weaponize it with speech codes and bowdlerized language so that the words needed to express the blindingly obvious facts of the matter are no longer accessible to us.

ChatGPT, with its well-documented refusal to countenance the unpleasant or the disturbing, offers a glimpse of how this world of bogus non-conformity, of bureaucrats who think they are Spartacus, will be ordered.

AS A COUNTER-FACTUAL, imagine that trauma was not the epicenter of both Woke and "anti-racist" politics. Were that the case, the moral would cede pride of place to the material and the psychic slights that so obsess those drawn to identity politics would be overshadowed by the macro-aggressions of class. In those circumstances, one of the most common rhetorical tropes of the identarian world—the person of color saying that they are 'tired'—would be seen for the moral preening that it is. Tired compared to a home health attendant, a person in a homeless shelter, a factory worker? The suggestion would be so ridiculous and, more to the point, so morally untenable. It is only by ignoring the material and, crucially, making it possible for the larger society to ignore them too, that identarian militancy can remain the center of attention.

Examples of this abound. When the Black Law Students Association at Georgetown demanded that Ilys Shapiro, a law professor at the school, be fired for having attacked President Biden's decision to only consider black women jurists as candidates to replace retiring US Supreme Court Justice Stephen Breyer, they did so on the grounds of the moral harm that exposure to this language had caused them. They were at the end of their rope, the students said, exhausted by the aggressions they were facing. One student even demanded a 'safe space' for them to cry. And although it seems highly unlikely that Georgetown will accede to the students' demands to fire Professor Shapiro, the controversy was by far the most important, and the most time-consuming, both for the students themselves and the Georgetown University administration that had occurred this year.

But where the counter-factual comes in is if one looks at Washington, DC (where Georgetown is situated) and asks whether—even granting that the students' claim of psychological harm is unassailable—of all the harms suffered by black people in Washington, DC in academic year 2021–2, this the gravest one. Even the students themselves might accept that the answer to that question is 'no'; indeed, they might angrily insist on the negative. And yet it is Professor Shapiro's supposedly racist remarks that mobilized them—not the condition of the black poor, not homelessness, etc.

To be sure, the young are self-absorbed, not to say worse. But this does not seem to me at the root of the contrast between a willingness to expend huge efforts to protest psychological harm and the undeniably much lesser willingness to protest material harm. Rather, what has happened is that the therapeutic culture—now weaponized politically as traumatic culture—has instilled in modern US society (and in many other parts of the world, increasingly not just in the Anglosphere but in much of Western Europe and even Latin America that are also beginning to see the same dialectic unfold), the idea that the psychological is absolutely equal—if not superior—to the material.

It is easy to accuse the identarians of being trivial. But this, I'm convinced, does them a deep injustice. For when 'just memory' (the expression is that of the Vietnamese-American writer and academic Viet Thanh Nguyen) is considered the prerequisite to a more equitable future, the moral hierarchy simply looks different. And, from this perspective, it is anything but a moral solecism for the psychological wounds of the past to be given priority over the material wounds of the present. But it *is* a moral solecism. Even conceding 'just memory' is a coherent moral ambition—and, further, an attainable one—all the acknowledgment of the past cannot assuage the sufferings of the present—unless, that is, such 'just memory' is accompanied by an idea not just of a psychological healed (that is to say, more just and equitable society psychically) but of a more just society materially. And that is all but completely absent in any serious way from the identarian wave that is now washing over us and, culturally at least, drowning us.

DUKE UNIVERSITY PRESS has published *Marx for Cats: A Radical Bestiary*[1] by Leigh Claire La Berge, a professor at the City University of New York. The gambit of the book, Professor La Berge writes, "is that the history of Western Capitalism can be told through the cat and that doing so reveal a heretofore unrecognized animality at the heart of Marx's critique." Cats, it seems, "have long been creatures of economic critique and communist possibility." However, Professor LaBerge insists, "a specter is haunting Marxism, the specter of the cat and the time has come for a feline critique, both of capitalism and of Marxism."[2]

It would be pleasant to imagine that Professor LaBerge was mounting an elaborate Alan Sokol-style prank (including on Duke University Press), but this is anything but the case. To the contrary—guess what?—the joke's on us: she is in deadly earnest. There is even a video on MarxforCats.com in which La Berge in all seriousness explains key Marxian concepts to an audience of cats, going so far as to pose questions to them such as "What is a commodity?", and then, "Is art a commodity?" At one point, she even reads them a passage from Marx's text, "Bourgeois Revolutions."

The fact that, self-evidently, the cats do not answer her queries does not seem to trouble Professor La Berge anymore than it seems to have troubled Duke University Press. What would a generation ago have been called 'delusional' (the stuff people in lunatic asylums who imagined themselves to be Christ or Cleopatra did or said) is now considered cutting edge critical theory (Professor La Berge's academic specialty, in fact). The true revolutionary, Professor LaBerge writes, approvingly quoting Che Guevara, "is guided by a great feeling of love." But, she adds,

> For too long, cats, indeed all animals, have been excluded from the reach of that loving, revolutionary embrace.[3]

Her aim is nothing less, she declares, than to realize Marxism's "potential to become an interspecies project." If ever there were a demonstration of what one sardonic person on X, who styles herself 'Uppity Witch,' and tweets at @senjii2022, has called the "deep vein of puerile immaturity that drives modern culture," it is *Marx for Cats.* And yet, increasingly, that is precisely what not only the humanities within the academe have become, but also what the culture in general has become: a subsidized play pen in which those within its confines produce nothing so productive as a sand castle, but instead deliver their daft fancies with a passionate conviction born of the belief that theirs is not just a but the emancipatory project of our time. I do not see how such a culture can be saved, nor any earthly reason why it should be mourned, and only hope to live long enough to assist at its funeral rites.

THE TWO MOST POWERFUL ELEMENTS of Woke are its project of moralizing everything (this is what makes it so clearly post-Protestant), and its project of politicizing everything. About the latter—to use a favorite Woke expression—there are no safe spaces for the non-political for the simple reason that such a category is held not to exist, or to be a mask for the politics of racial supremacy, patriarchy, and exploitation that Woke is trying to overthrow. What this is already doing, and will continue to do, to the pursuit of pleasure is one of the more interesting questions posed by Woke. 'Check your privilege' is no longer enough. At the cutting edge of gender militancy, it is increasingly common to find the idea of 'check your preference'—that is, to ask yourself whether not wanting to sleep with someone (as in the case, for example, of a heterosexual man or a lesbian not wanting to have sex with a trans woman with a penis) is an act of transphobia.

What informs all this on the deepest level is, I think, the belief that not only is being a good person more important than anything else, but that personal goodness is, fundamentally, a political act. Unsurprisingly, this is now rampant in the liberal professions, and has now migrated into the STEM world, to the point where a white female physician some years ago agonized in the pages of *The New England Journal of Medicine* that, "If we white physicians are to heal others and ultimately the health care system, we must first heal ourselves."[1]

That this physician wants to virtue signal in this exhibitionistic way is her business. But what is new and harmful in all this is the metaphorization of the idea of healing, in that it erases any useful distinction between being good at what one does and being a good person. To put it starkly, this doctor—being by her own auto-diagnosis in need of being healed—healing herself of her racism is not remotely as important as treating one of her patients for leukaemia. And yet, she seems to think the reverse is the case. "If we white physicians are to heal others [...]," she writes, "we must *first* heal ourselves" (emphasis mine).

The problem is that this gets things exactly backwards: not only is it possible, but it is far more important, for a physician to heal a child's leukaemia than to tend to her own racism. It is the difference between heal and 'heal,' but so complete has the triumph of metaphor been in this society that the distinction literally no longer informs adult judgment. Meanwhile, it is apparently unbearable to the moral sensibilities of this age to accept the fact that it is perfectly possible for a racist person to make a scientific discovery that is of benefit to humanity. Instead, though, the contemporary tendency is to claim that, if bad people seem to be able to do something better than good people, the problem must be with the definition of doing something better. Thus, if the cell biologist David Sabatini is thought guilty of sexual misconduct, that trumps any contribution he might have made and he should have his lab taken away from him. But, since that leaves begging the question of the importance of that contribution, the response is to think that the idea of genius is hierarchical nonsense and that, therefore, firing someone who is deemed to have behaved immorally and oppressively will do science no significant harm.

Another expression of this moralization is the relaxation of testing requirements and, even, as in a recent case, the sacking of a science professor considered by his students (and presumably by his university's administration as well) to have been too severe a grader. But given the present ethos, it could hardly be otherwise. Perhaps we may know from sports that being good at something and being a good person have little to do with each other. But, for the moment at least, the pressure to pretend this does not apply to medicine or physics or, for that matter, sculpture and poetry is all but irresistible. If we judge people on their goodness rather than their fitness—or, to put it another way, if their goodness *is* their fitness—then to reject someone on the basis of their grades is an affront to *their* humanity, just as to accept someone despite their moral affronts (real or imagined) is an affront to *our* humanity.

It seems obvious that we are entering full-speed a world whose good intentions will destroy what is good about this civilization without improving the many things that are cruel and monstrous about it.

THE PHRASE "EVERYONE IS SPECIAL" may be the most radical single utterance of the current cultural convulsion of the Anglosphere. It was actually the title (and refrain) of a song first sung in 2005 in the final episode of *Barney & Friends*, a then hugely popular television show whose target audience was small children—that is, children who, as was said back in the era when adults did not want to be little more than overgrown children with sex lives and money (which is to say all previous eras), everyone understood not to yet have reached the age of reason. A claim made to toddlers, its greatest success is in infantilizing those who utter it. Of course, as a linguistic claim, it makes no sense. For, if everyone is 'special' then no one is 'ordinary,' in which case why keep the word 'special' at all? And while one is at it, surely in a world where everyone is beautiful—the other feel-good commonplace of this culture—there is no longer any need for the word 'beauty.'

It is to the lyrics of that sickly sweet song from *Barney* that this culture is committing intellectual suicide. But then, what other option does it have? For, once the belief that we are all special and that we are all beautiful can no longer be challenged, then the inescapable corollary must be that we are all brilliant as well—in our own way, of course: diversity, always diversity. This conviction is already coming to dominate the educational establishment, above all in K–12. No one must get a failing grade; indeed, they must get a superlative grade or just be assumed not to require being graded at all. Because, given how special, and beautiful, and intelligent all students are, to proceed in any other way would be the height of injustice.

It will not end there: the workplace will be next, since this and subsequent generations that grew up being told everything it did was marvelous will have great trouble reconciling itself to being told in the workplace that they are to be judged on the basis of their actual performance. That said, the crisis is likely to be a short-lived one. In the age of AI, there will quite simply be fewer and fewer workplaces still largely staffed by human beings, large numbers of whom, for their part, are likely to find themselves beautiful, and special...and out of a job. Hollywood scriptwriters and the staffers at media companies are already discovering this. And at the rate things are going, by comparison, at least, the gig economy is going to seem humane. But where all this starts is with the debasement of language or, more precisely, the crushing of linguistic realism in the name of a euphemism-dependent utopianism. For, without language there can be no reason, and without reason there can no future—no decent one, anyway.

BLAKE BAILEY, THE AUTHOR OF a very fine biography of John Cheever—who also recently published the authorized biography of Philip Roth—stands accused by a number of his former female students of 'grooming' them when, during the 1990s, he was an eighth grade teacher at New Orleans' Lusher Middle School.[1] 'Grooming' in this context means pursuing eroticized, but not physical, sexual relationships with underage girls which will 'set the table' for the 'groomer' to pursue sexual relationships with them once they came of age. Bailey has denied these charges and, though he conceded in an email to one former student that his behavior had been "deplorable," he was insistent he had done nothing "illegal."[2]

The story was first broken by Ed Champion, a sometime playwright and novelist of indifferent success who, in contrast, was well-known as a host of a radio 'something' called the *Bat Segundo Show*, and is now a prolific blogger, on his (apparently all-too-appropriately-named) site, edrants.com. I was unaware of Champion until the Blake Bailey controversy erupted, but from what I have read since—including the braggadocio on his own website—I find him odious in the extreme. Champion has himself been accused of harassment of different kinds, including of threatening people he has taken a dislike to, or feels slighted by in some way, by revealing some secret of theirs unless they apologize to him. He has denied these accusations but anyone wanting to see what sort of character he appears to be should read the devastating piece Laura Miller did on him in *Salon* in 2014.[3] Champion's own account of himself—which is obviously the diametrical opposite of

Miller's—can be found on the About/Contacts page of his blog "Reluctant Habits."[4]

I have no idea if the accusations made against Bailey are true or false. What interests me is that, despite nothing yet having been proven against him, Bailey has in the course of a couple of days been fired by his literary agency, The Story Factory, which announced that it had terminated its association with him "immediately after we learned of the disturbing allegations."[5] Bailey's publisher, W. W. Norton, was equally quick to distance themselves from him, announcing that, not only would it stop promoting the Roth biography, but it was also halting further shipments of copies of it to booksellers and wholesalers—this even though the biography is already on the best-seller lists. This would continue, Norton said in a statement, pending any further information that may emerge.

Again: Bailey may be guilty of everything that the women who have come forward accuse him of. But neither his literary agency nor his publisher are making any such claim. Quite the contrary: both The Story Factory's and Norton's public announcements about the matter are entirely straightforward in saying that they just don't know. The Story Factory speaks of having terminated Bailey because of "disturbing *allegations*"[6] [italics mine], while the Norton statement speaks of halting promotion and distribution pending any information that *may* emerge [again, italics mine]. In other words, far from being a presumption of innocence, as obviously there would have to be in a court of law—but also until not so long ago would have governed a literary agency's or a publisher's relationship with an author accused of wrongdoing—there is a *de facto* presumption of the author's guilt.

In effect, even though such language does not normally—indeed if ever—appear in an agency agreement or publishing contract with a writer of literary fiction or non-fiction, what both The Story Factory and Norton have done is retroactively and unilaterally impose a morals clause on their respective agreements with Bailey. This is standard practice in, for example, the sponsorship contracts famous athletes are offered by sporting goods manufacturers. One law firm that specializes in such agreements has on its website an example of what it calls a 'strict' morals clause, defined as one that would stipulate—and the language repays reading in full—that "if at any time, in the opinion of Sponsor, Athlete becomes the subject of public disrepute, contempt, or scandal that affects Athlete's image or goodwill, then Company may, upon written notice to Athlete, immediately suspend or terminate this Endorsement Agreement and Athlete's services hereunder, in addition to any other rights and remedies that Sponsor may have hereunder or at law or in equity."[7]

What is key here is that such contracts do not say that the sponsor is permitted to break its agreement with the athlete only if he or she has been shown to have done something wrong but, rather, that if the athlete's reputation is tarnished, even if the accusations against him or her turn out to be completely baseless, the sponsor is completely within its rights to sever all ties and suspend or terminate any contractual arrangement that exists. This is precisely what The Story Factory agency has done. Bailey may not be guilty, but there is no doubt that the accusations against him have for now created a scandal. So Norton is doing what any sponsor would have the right to do: suspend their contract with Bailey until, in effect, the dust settles.

There is another word for this: censorship. For, writers are not sports figures, and publishers and literary agencies are not—or at least *were* not—commercial sponsors. That this distinction appears not to have any importance, either for The Story Factory or for Norton, is an emblem of the moralistic mindlessness of the times. And, in my view, anyone who believes that this cultural moment in which censorship has regained its centrality and self-righteousness again and has become the default position of the American cultural establishment will end any time soon is deluding themselves. Instead, we are entering a Woke version of the Victorian Age, or post-Hays Code Hollywood, in which censorship will be the norm, not the exception.

With historical perspective, there is nothing particularly surprising about this. After all, those who had been adults in the late-eighteenth century never really adapted to the moralism of the nineteenth century. That's what Talleyrand meant when he said that those who had not lived before the French Revolution had not known the sweetness of life. It took the First World War to break the Victorian moral consensus. My suspicion is that the increasing consensus that a writer or an artist's moral character, and political and increasingly racial and gender bona fides, should determine whether they are published or exhibited, celebrated or ignored, will grow stronger, not weaker, in the decades to come. Obviously, the internet makes it possible to publish or exhibit one's work, so, *technically*, one is not being censored. But the traditional venues still hold sway in the cultural-academic-philanthropic complex, and will, I think, for the foreseeable future. And in those contexts, morals clauses, whether *de facto* or *de jure*, will become commonplace. It will, after all, all be done in the name of elementary decency and compassion for and solidarity with victims. Nothing surprising there either: censorship has always claimed the moral warrant of being undertaken for the greater good.

THE DISCLOSURE THAT THE WORKS of the celebrated children's book writer Roald Dahl, —of *Matilda, Charlie and the Chocolate Factory*, and *The Witches* fame—have been systematically purged of language that could be deemed offensive to the sensibilities of the enlightened bourgeoise of the Anglosphere, probably should come as no surprise.[1] Ours is not only the second great age of Bowdlerization,[2] and the rationales Thomas, Jane, and Henrietta Bowdler offered when they presented their Family Shakespeare in 1807 are virtually indistinguishable from those being offered now by the Puffin imprint of Random House/Penguin and by the Roald Dahl Estate for their comprehensive defanging and moral 'sanitizing' of Dahl's work.

In both cases, the stated goal has not been to consign either Shakespeare or Dahl to the dustbin of (literary) history but, instead, to *save* each of those authors from such an ignoble fate by editing and rewriting their works in such a way as to allow contemporary readers—who might otherwise rightly take offense and as a result abstain from reading, say, *Hamlet* or *James and the Giant Peach*—to continue doing so with a clear moral conscience. As Thomas Bowdler put it in his preface to the 1819 edition of *The Family Shakespeare*:

> My great objects in this undertaking are to remove from the writings of Shakespeare some defects which diminish their value, and at the same time to present to the public an edition of his plays which the parent, the guardian, and the instructor of youth may place, without fear, in the hands of his pupil; and from which the

> pupil may derive instruction, as well as pleasure; may improve his moral principles while he refines his taste; and, without incurring the danger of being hurt with any indelicacy of expression [...][3]

This not only meant dealing with what the Bowdlers called Shakespeare's "indelicacies of expression" by either omitting them altogether or replacing them with something more palatable to a family audience (for example, the Bowdler's replaced Shakespeare's 'God' and 'Jesu' with 'Heavens') but, also, cutting immoral characters such as the prostitute Dorothy "Doll" Tearsheet from *Henry IV*, Part Two, or else rewriting scenes so as not to offend the moral sensitivities of the time, as in the case of Ophelia's death in *Hamlet*, which the Bowdler changes from a suicide to an accidental drowning.

The Bowdler understood—and explicitly presented—their project as one of reducing Shakespeare from himself, to separate the transcendent wheat of his work from the indecent and immoral chaff that marred. "The language is not always faultless," Thomas Bowdler wrote in the 1819 preface.

> Many words and expressions occur which are of so indecent Nature as to render it highly desirable that they should be erased. Of these, the greater part were evidently introduced to gratify the bad taste of the age in which he lived, and the rest may perhaps be ascribed to his own unbridled fancy. But neither the vicious taste of the age nor the most brilliant effusions of wit can afford an excuse for profaneness or obscenity; and if these can be obliterated, the transcendent genius of the poet would

undoubtedly shine with more unclouded lustre.[4]

All of these justifications for rewriting Shakespeare—that his work suffered from being suffused by the unacceptable views of his era that reading offensive passages would both offend readers and harm them morally and, thus, rewriting his work was the greatest service one could render it—are now being offered by Penguin Random House and the Dahl Estate as the rationale for the changes they have made to Dahl's work. These changes, the publisher announced, were being made so that, "the wonderful words of Roald Dahl can transport you to different worlds and introduce you to the most marvellous characters."[5] But, just as Thomas Bowdler had argued that the indecent language (and presumably scenes) in Shakespeare had been introduced to "gratify the bad taste of the age" and his (presumably negative) "unbridled fancy," so Dahl had written his books "many years ago," and as a result the publisher needed to "regularly review the language to ensure that it can continue to be enjoyed by all today."[6]

Just as *The Family Shakespeare* had as its most important ambition being a version of Shakespeare to which parents, guardians, and teachers could safely expose children, so a Penguin Random House representative told the British trade publication *The Bookseller* that, since "children as young as five or six read Roald Dahl books, and often they are the first stories they will read independently,"[7] Dahl's publisher was burdened with "a significant responsibility," particularly "as it might be the first time [these children] are navigating written content without a parent, teacher or carer." The publisher denied that any of this should be viewed as distorting Dahl's work. To the contrary, Francesca Dow, head of Penguin Random House's Children's Book Division, proclaimed that Dahl had long been, and remained, her favorite author. Her favorite memories of reading to her children when they were small, she said, were reading them Dahl.

There being apparently no Bowdlers in-house at Penguin Random House, the publisher had turned to outside sensitivity readers—an increasingly common practice in English-language publishing across the Anglosphere—by hiring a company called Inclusive Minds to suggest changes. In a long statement to *The Hollywood Reporter* in response to the paper's questions about the group's involvement in the Dahl rewrites, Inclusive Minds denied that they were sensitivity readers but, instead, had the goal of connecting publishers with its network of "inclusion ambassadors," young readers with "many different lived experiences who are willing to share their insight [with publishers and authors] to help them in the process of creating authentically—and often incidentally—inclusive books"[8] during the process of writing and editing. Older titles—like Dahl's books—were "not the main focus for the Ambassadors." Instead, Inclusive Minds took the view that "better authenticity is achieved through input at development stages."

Of course, this account of how books get written is, actually, a description of how film and television scripts get written—*not* books. For, it is clear that, in the Inclusive Minds model, while the author is part of the process, it is very much in the way the author of the first draft of a script is part of the process—that is, as the producer of a text that then needs to be shaped by editors, perhaps even by other writers, and checked for possible offensive content, just as most scripts produced for major film companies are. Even here, Inclusive Minds' claim that it is not an organization of sensitivity readers rings more than a bit hollow. But where what the group is pleased to call "older titles" are concerned, it is a distinction without a difference. As the statement to *The Hollywood Reporter* stated, the group believed "better authenticity is achieved through input at development stages" (the film and TV script model again).

> We do think those with lived experience can provide valuable input when it comes to reviewing language that can be damaging and perpetuate harmful stereotypes. In all our work with marginalised young people, the very real negative impact and damage caused to self-worth and mental health from biased, stereotypical and inauthentic representation is a recurring theme. On any project, it's the role of the ambassador to help identify language and portrayals that could be inauthentic or problematic, and to highlight why, as well as indicate potential solutions. The publisher (and/or author) then have all the information to make informed decisions regarding what changes they wish to make to manuscripts and illustrations.[9]

Obviously, "indicating potential solutions" is exactly what sensitivity readers do, as even the briefest perusal of statements by sensitivity readers and books about the process makes clear. And Inclusive Minds has never denied the claims of Penguin Random House and the Dahl Estate that the changes that were eventually made were done in collaboration with the group and as a result of its suggestions. But if Inclusive Minds was being somewhat disingenuous when initially announcing the changes that had been made, Dahl's publisher and his Estate at first were being entirely so. The changes, they insisted, amounted only to "a relatively small number of textual edits,"[10] though the company left itself an out by adding that the textual changes were "minimal" within "*the context of the word count of the wider books*" [italics mine]. It quickly became clear that, whatever their relation was to the word count, the changes were anything but minimal.

To the contrary, as *The Daily Telegraph* laid out in detail, a systematic effort had been made to eliminate everything that might offend the sensibilities, not of children—as with *The Family Shakespeare*, these exercises in moral censorship are always undertaken to please parents and teachers—but of adults. As Dahl's biographer, Matthew Dennison, put it, Dahl never,

> had any truck with librarians who criticised his books as too frightening, lacking moral role models, negative in their portrayal of women, etc. Dahl wrote stories intended to kindle in children a lifelong love of reading and to remind them of the childhood wonderlands of magic and enchantment, aims in which he succeeded triumphantly. Adult anxieties about political niceties didn't register in this outlook. This said, although Dahl could be unabashed in offending adults, he took pains never to alienate or make unhappy his child readers.[11]

And he added,

> "I don't give a b----r what grown-ups think," was a characteristic statement [of Dahl's]. And I'm almost certain that he would have recognized that alterations to his novels prompted by the political climate were driven by adults rather than children, and this always inspired derision, if not contempt, in Dahl.[12]

The changes tick all the boxes of contemporary high bourgeois—or as we would say today 'professional managerial'—class pieties, just as the Bowdlers ticked those of nineteenth-century high bourgeois Britain. Not just all mockery of fat people, but all mention of fatness as a physical state, is quite simply eliminated so that, for example, in *The Enormous Crocodile*, "fat juicy little child" becomes "juicy little child;" in *Fantastic Mr Fox*, "he was enormously fat" becomes "he was enormous;" and in *The Witches*, even mice are not allowed to be fat and so "fat little brown mouse" is changed to "little brown mouse." In addition, every reference to what would now be called a binary conception of gender is disallowed. Thus, in *Matilda*, "mothers and fathers" becomes "parents," in *George's Marvelous Medicine*, "he didn't have a brother or sister" becomes "he didn't have any siblings," and in *James and the Giant Peach*, "the Cloud-Men were all standing" becomes "the "Cloud-People were all standing."

Other potentially offensive characterizations have simply been removed. For example, Dahl's frequent descriptions of various characters in his books as 'crazy' are nowhere to be found. In *Charlie and The Chocolate Factory*, "the crazy prince" becomes "the prince," in *The Twits*, "mad" is changed to "dotty," and in *James and the Giant Peach*, a comment that "the boy's crazy" has simply been removed. Women are no longer ever referred to as ugly, and for some reason in several of the books "old hag" becomes "old crow," even though elsewhere pejorative references to animals, as in *James and the Giant Peach*, "don't be an ass" becomes "don't be so silly," and in *Matilda*, "wise old bird" becomes "wise teacher" (thus are anthropocentrism and ageism confounded in a single clause). At the same time, references to women holding menial jobs are replaced by them having superior ones. In *The Witches*, for example, "even if she is working as a cashier in a supermarket or typing letters for a businessman" is replaced by "even if she is working as a top scientist or running a business."[13]

More startling, still, are the times in which writers that Dahl mentions who are now considered racist or sexist are either eliminated or replaced by more acceptable authors. In *Matilda*, for example, "she went on olden-day sailing ships with Joseph Conrad. She went to Africa with Ernest Hemingway and to India with Rudyard Kipling" is replaced by "she went to nineteenth century estates with Jane Austen. She went to Africa with Ernest Hemingway and California with John Steinbeck." Elsewhere in that book, "Dickens or Kipling" becomes "Dickens or Austen."[14]

Taken in toto, Penguin Random House's claim that the purpose of the cuts and rewrites is so that "Dahl can continue to be enjoyed by all today" actually means "so that there is nothing in the new editions of Dahl likely to offend millennial parents or risk provoking a storm of criticism on social media."[15] In this sense, critiques of the revision that have appeared in the conservative press miss a central point. Did the Dahl Estate and Penguin Random House cave in to Woke pressure? Yes, of course they did. But caving into Woke pressure is good business and, now that the rights to Dahl's work have been bought by Netflix, better business still. And whether this was the calculus that informed the choices made by the publisher, by the Dahl Estate, and by Netflix, the commercial reality is that without edits—that is, without a repackaging that would once again stir public interest—Dahl's books would likely sell ever fewer copies as the decades rolled on, whereas now the downward trajectory has—as they say in business school—been 'disrupted' and new marketing possibilities opened. The same is true of the recently announced decision of the Ian Fleming Estate and Fleming's publishers to relaunch the James Bond books with many of the offensive bits removed.

One of the things the Dahl controversy exposes is the fundamental error of the anti-Woke: it is not that Woke is compatible with capitalism, as conservatives and non-Woke leftists have now understood; it is that it is of benefit to capitalism. And the fact that Penguin Random House appeared after the uproar over the Dahl revision to backtrack and agree to bring out the new editions and a separate 'classic' reissue with Dahl's original texts left intact is better business practice still: a market segment for the Woke and a market segment for the anti-Woke. What could be more remunerative?

Is the academic-cultural-philanthropic complex of the Anglosphere—of which publishing is an important component—stoned on its own virtue?

It would be more accurate to say it is stoned on its ethical ambitions. In doing so, it illustrates Roger Scruton's definition of Kitsch as relying "on codes and clichés that convert the higher emotions into a pre-digested and trouble-free form—the form that can be most easily pretended."[16] But it also converts them into the form that can most easily be sold. And, in a certain sense, the Dahl case teaches us as much, if not more, about this as it does about the subjugation of all wild writing—even though Dahl was wild, and the charges of racism that have long been leveled against him are absolutely true (and it is important to remember this even if one adamantly rejects what Penguin Random House has done)—to the dictates of the complacent pieties of the professional managerial classes of the Anglosphere.

As for the literary questions, so far these remain unanswered. In a brilliant essay on Dahl in *The New York Review of Books,* the brilliant Merve Emre—by far the most interesting of the new generation of literary critics and essays—fairly and forcefully revisits Dahl's racism and honors the efforts of Dahl's longtime American editor (in Dahl's lifetime) to rein in Dahl's most odious fantasies. She concludes by saying that there are far better children's book writers than either the unexpurgated or the expurgated Dahl for parents to turn to. I have no brief for Dahl—I am against him being rewritten; I am not for him—and I don't doubt she is correct. That said, it is precisely Dahl's cruelty and malice, the id made palpable in his prose, that in my view at least explains his attraction to children and perhaps the disgust he provokes in many parents (Emre is a far better guide than Francesca Dow in this regard). But, when Penguin Random House and the Dahl Estate insist that in the revised editions of Dahl they wanted to retain what they call his mischievousness while jettisoning the maliciousness, I wonder if that is possible—just as I wonder if a children's literature purged of its malice in the name of a better, more just world, and a kinder, more inclusive, less violent language (to be clear, here I am not using these words ironically in any way, shape, or form), will be of any lasting appeal to the 'Lord of the Flies' side of children, which, like it or not, almost all of them have to a greater or lesser extent.

ROBERT HUGHES WROTE THAT, "One of the first conditions of freedom is to discover the line beyond which politics may not go, and literature is one of the means by which the young (and old) find this out."[1] But virtually the entire project of literature in the contemporary Anglosphere has become that of erasing this line. And any work of literature that is not political is suspect—or, more precisely, since the claim is that all literature is political—like everything else in life—novelists and poets who do not accept that their work is political are, in doing so, offering proof of their own and of their work's reactionary politics. But, in reality, most of the politicized literature of today—so much of which fails miserably even to attain the level of decent, old-fashioned agit-prop—is made up of disguised autobiographies by people whose fascination with themselves is more a manifestation of their powerlessness than of their emancipation. How they will be able to face their own mortality is a question I often puzzle over.

IT SHOULD BE OBVIOUS BY NOW that the DEI statements that are increasingly required at the meetings of professional associations are the functional equivalents of the loyalty oaths of the 1950s. What is more interesting is the degree to which the entire academic-cultural-philanthropic complex is now committed in practical terms to effectively discourage any scholarship other than that of scholarship with a social mission. This is not anti-Woke hyperbole. Applications for tenure, decisions by professional associations as to which papers to allow to be presented at annual meetings, etc., are now graded both according to more traditional criteria of academic merit and interest, but also for their contribution to 'anti-racism,' (usually defined nowadays largely along the lines of the work of Ibram X. Kendi).

But, in my view, while the intellectual stranglehold that Kendi, Nikole Hannah-Jones, and other like-minded polemicists (scholars would be a misnomer, despite the plush academic posts many of them hold) has had a noxious effect on the cultural and scholarly institutions of the Anglosphere, the graver moral, cultural, and intellectual effects of the hegemony of the DEI mindset has little to do with these figures. Their influence will wane. But the DEI framework itself is unlikely to; it is likely to endure even when, or if, it jettisons demotic Critical Race Theory à la Kendi or à Robin DiAngelo. This is because what has been broken beyond repair in academe and in the museum is the idea that any work that cannot justify itself on the basis of its contribution to political and social emancipation is inherently less valuable to work than can claim to make such a contribution. In other words, everything must be politicized and moralized, which means that the apolitical is now taken as morally and intellectually suspect, if not illicit.

Such an assumption is likely to prevail not least because, while the right is largely opposed to Woke, it too largely rejects the legitimacy of the apolitical. One must be careful here: to make this claim is emphatically not to say that no great art can be produced under such conditions. Andrei Sinyavsky's *On Socialist Realism*, is dispositive on this point. "Art is not afraid of dictatorship, severity, repressions, or even conservatism and clichés," he wrote.

> When necessary, art can be narrowly religious, dumbly governmental, devoid of individuality—and yet good. We go into aesthetic raptures over the stereotypes of Egyptian art, Russian icons, and folklore. Art is elastic enough to fit into any bed of Procrustes that history presents to it.[1]

But can the same be said about thought? My suspicion is that Sinyavsky would have responded in the affirmative. I myself am less sure. For, the hegemony of the DEI mindset in the institutions of the professional managerial classes of the Anglosphere not only is a machine for activating the censor inside one's own head (how could this not be so, if one's professional advancement depends on it), but just as dangerously—to thought, to art, I mean—it activates not only a conformist mindset but, even worse perhaps, a bureaucratic one. Has one ticked all the right boxes, etc.? Within conformity, there is still room for manoeuvre: that is why the 'loyalty oath' aspect of

DEI seems far less consequential to me than its bureaucratizing side. It was perhaps more difficult (I am not certain) but nonetheless perfectly possible to do good work in the context of compulsory chapel, or McCarthyite loyalty oaths. But is it possible to do good work when the concept of non-political work has been repudiated and declared a moral affront in that it is a roadblock to the emancipation of humanity? That, I very much doubt. First the political was the political, then the personal was the political, and now everything is the political. The result of this has been that everything is now moralized and this in turn means you need the soft equivalent of a morals police to enforce these dicta: after all, one can't let immorality run rampant. It is the same mentality that gives rise to the real morals police in places like Iran, but without the violence, and with a smile.

THE GUARDIAN REPORTS that New Zealand's Arts Council has pulled funding for a Shakespeare festival that for three decades had sponsored productions of Shakespeare's plays by secondary school students, on the grounds that the program "did not demonstrate the relevance to the contemporary art context of Aotearoa in this time and place and landscape," and that "the genre was located within a canon of imperialism and missed the opportunity to create a living curriculum and show relevance."[1] The Arts Council grant represents ten percent of the festival annual budget so the festival will survive. But this story is emblematic of the ongoing process of cultural self-mutilation mistaking itself for emancipation that is taking place across the Anglosphere.

Whatever was wrong with 'Art for Art's Sake,' it was infinitely preferable to the current cultural conventional wisdom, which is that art that does not serve the moral and political ambitions of the present is either irrelevant—as the New Zealand Arts Council's statement states explicitly several times—or, actually, an obstacle to such ambitions—as in the reference to "the canon of imperialism."

Such a worldview cannot distinguish between the art itself, and the history of its uses. This explains the crisis in classics departments in the universities of the English-speaking world: militant young scholars look at the uses Classical Greek and Imperial Rome were put to by Western imperialism and find this much more interesting than Rome and Greece taken in their own right. On this logic, to claim that studying these effects may not be the province of classics departments at all, and certainly should not be its principal concern, is to become complicit in that imperial project.

The New Zealand Arts Council is making the same argument. Shakespeare "exists within a canon of imperialism,"[2] which—as in the case of the imperialist use of the classics—is obviously true historically, and therefore it is not just irrelevant to the present, it is toxic to the (desired) future.

And, if you accept the idea that art has two purposes—to represent communities, whether these communities be racial, ethnic, gender, etc., and to contribute in the present to the fashioning of the future—then the Arts Council decision is indeed perfectly logical. In the same article we learn that Nicola Hyland, a professor of drama at the University of Wellington, told *The Guardian* that she believed Shakespeare was "over-represented" in the country. "It would be a massive, awesome act of decolonization if we discovered our own stories first and discovered Shakespeare afterwards,"adding,

> Wouldn't it be great if young people could come home and say, 'Hey, Mum, Dad, I just found this story and it's really similar to Hinemoa and Tūtānekai. It's Romeo and Juliet'.[3]

Leaving aside the fact that Shakespeare's plots are the least interesting thing about his work, and that even assuming the plots of both works are indeed similar, there is where the similarity ends. This is the vision of art and artists as representatives of their peoples, what the great and problematic Mexican politician, philosopher, and cultural theorist, meant when he wrote, "For my people, my spirit will speak."[4] It is this entirely sociologized and mobilized vision of art, a mix of folklore and agit-prop in which the repressed past (by imperialism, racism, patriarchy, etc.) and the radiant future are all that matter.

That Shakespeare didn't 'speak' for white Europeans, anymore than the great sixth century Sanskrit poet Bharavi's *Kirtrjunya* 'spoke' for India, should be self-evident. And yet it is now completely incomprehensible to the academic-cultural-philanthropic complex of the Anglosphere: real art, art that inspires across time and space, and can enchant, move, sadden, and delight people who could not be further away from Elizabethan England or the Western Ganga dynasty is too dangerous, too autonomous, too uncontrollable—which is why it is so threatening to the cultural apparatchiks of the contemporary Anglosphere. And that's why they are trying, and too often succeeding, in strangling it.

WRITERS ARE INCREASINGLY being pushed to hire so-called 'sensitivity readers' whose job, in effect, is to be moral fact-checkers. These sensitivity readers are there to catch and warn their author-clients about what the travel writer and commentator Monisha Rajesh described in *The Guardian* as "offensive content."[1] Rajeesh insisted in her piece that, "No one is policing imaginations or telling authors what they should and shouldn't write about." This might be true of Rajesh herself but it is certainly not true of many others on her side of the debate. In any case, this is wholly disingenuous on her part for, even if she is not telling authors *what* they should write about something or someone in a novel, she is telling authors *how* they should do so. And she more-or-less admits as much when in the very next sentence she adds that, "We owe each other due diligence before we set out to write."

Writing in the British *Bookseller*, the writer and editor Tara Tobler praises writers of color for "step[ping] up to say how white Enlish [sic] could be made more compassionate, more intelligent, more accurate."[2] "Why on earth," demands Tobler (who is white herself), "aren't we saying thank you?" And she goes on to say that,

> [i]nclusionary language is there because racist language is a failure. Ethically and aesthetically it fails. *It causes trauma* [italics mine]. It's reductive. It's riddled with clichés.[3]

With mock astonishment, she concludes: "why anyone would fight to hang onto it, I don't know."

That Tobler does not like what she calls "the white novel," believing it to be "plagued by paralysis and narcissism" precisely because it rejects the moral reformation of "white English," is her business. But, when she writes that for white writers and publishers to "refuse the work of anti-racism is both to fail to understand ourselves as we exist within the world, and the world in its true complexity," is by [her] definition also to "refuse to write or publish well," she is presenting a wholly politicized vision of what literature does. The same revolting Woke and Kendi/DiAngelo-style binary (white/non-white) is what Tobler is offering her fellow writers and editors. Literature that is inclusive and anti-racist is good; literature that is not, is bad. Literature—to use a word Tobler employs a number of times in her piece—must have a message to be any good. And not any message, mind: the morally right message. So much, among other things, abstraction.

The abject absurdity of the notion of 'white English' should be self-evident, even though, if it existed at all (which it does not) this binary would require excluding non-white novelists such as Ellison or Naipaul, or poets such as Walcott, who wrote in such 'unreformed' English. But Tobler speaks for many young writers and editors in the English-speaking world, and that is what makes her arguments—like those of Monisha Rajesh—so destructive, as racist essentialism always is. But, given how widely this view has spread in the Anglosphere, it is hardly surprising that 'sensitivity readers' are in increasing demand, both from (white) authors, and, equally increasingly, from publishers. For, if writing well by definition means being inclusive, being anti-racist, etc.—then, of course, writers would want to secure for themselves what I called earlier such 'moral fact-checking.'

What I find most startling in all this is the romanticization of the writer or artist's vocation, the refusal to admit that a great deal of the literature from the past that has lasted has been immoral or amoral. But in 2021, this will not do. Just as the Victorians out of sexual prudery tried to cover even the legs of pianos, so twenty-first century Victorians such as Rajesh and Tobler are trying out of a new kind of politicized moral prudery sailing under the flag of anti-racism and inclusivity (not to mention under medicalized fetishization of trauma) to impose the claim that only morally defensible art is acceptable art.

IT IS REPORTED THAT the University of Northampton in the UK has put a trigger warning on Orwell's *1984*. This came out thanks to reporting in the *Daily Mail*,[1] which ran the story as one more example of Woke running amok in Britain. And to some extent, this is certainly the case. But what is interesting is that this move is less about Woke and more about the triumph of a therapeutic culture where the threat of a student being traumatized from being exposed to a work of art with no advance warning of the psychic dangers that it depicts could mean that there is potential risk everywhere: the library and, indeed, the streaming service as psychic minefield.

Were the trigger warning only being applied to Orwell (who, by the way, is now excoriated on the Woke left and idolized on the right), then thinking in terms of Woke politics might, indeed, be warranted. But the *Daily Mail* story goes on to inform us that the University of Northampton has also slapped trigger warnings on Samuel Beckett's play *Endgame*, the graphic novel *V For Vendetta* by Alan Moore and David Lloyd, and Jeanette Winterson's *Sexing The Cherry*—all works far more associated with the left than the right.

It is, of course, true that all these works do have the potential to be "offensive and upsetting," in the words of the trigger warning to students. But that, of course, is the point—or one of them, anyway—of all these works. We now find ourselves in the world not of ethical scruple but of psychic denial, of the fantasy that students in particular—and, presumably, society as a whole—have the right to be protected from even inadvertent exposure to anything that might upset them.

They may, obviously, ignore the trigger warnings, but that does not vitiate an institution like the University of Northampton having the moral obligation to provide them. Utter fragility: the new normal.

TRIGGER WARNINGS HAVE an interesting history. They derive from medical research into post-traumatic stress disorder (PTSD) that suggested—as summarized in a National Institute of Mental Health flyer on the subject—that it can be triggered by re-experiencing "words, objects, or situations that are reminders of the event," often provoking intense fear.[1] At first, the term was used fairly narrowly, largely in the context of victims of rape and sexual abuse. But, in a culture fundamentally grounded in therapeutic and 'metaphorized' understandings of the world, one in which there is no fundamental valid distinction to be made between the *psyche* and the *soma*, it was inevitable that the contexts in which trigger warnings would be considered imperative would expand rapidly, above all on university campuses across the Anglosphere.

Although there is ample disagreement about how narrow or expansive they should be, for those who are convinced about the need for trigger warnings—and their corollary: campus bans on hate speech, which includes barring speakers from outside, professors, and student groups believed to traffic in it—two arguments are regularly adduced. The first is scientific evidence that verbal aggression can cause stress similar to that triggered by physical aggression and some forms of sexual abuse, so that if you are chronically stressed, the triggering words will add to that threat and, sooner or later, imperil your physical health. This is what justifies the utterly far-fetched claim that the expression of opinions in a classroom, or the assignment of course materials, might not just offend students, but threaten their physical health.

The otherwise incomprehensible claim is that, for students to feel safe on campus, they must be protected (or at least be able to protect themselves) from stressful speech which may prove as harmful to their psychological health as a mugging, an act of sexual abuse, or even a rape would be to their physical health. This is why the DEI revolution that has led universities to commit themselves to being welcoming and inclusive environments for groups previously excluded or marginalized has come to be defined in the medicalized vocabulary of safety.

One might object that, even assuming one accepts the rejection in this context of any useful distinction between the psychological and the physical, this does not justify the reactions (or over-reactions, depending on your view) to seemingly trivial affronts, such as the 2021 showing in a class at the University of Michigan without trigger warnings of a film version of *Othello* in which Laurence Olivier plays the eponymous role in blackface, or, more generally, the concept of micro-aggressions—at first glance insignificant slights that are viewed as anything but insignificant instances of triggering verbal violence. The answer, according to the psychologist Lisa Feldman Barrett, who has helped popularize the idea that hateful speech is violence, is that no, in and of itself, the physiological effects of a single incident of hate speech may not have any physiological effect but that "is that if you are chronically stressed, the words are likely to pile on and add to that."[2]

And, in the view of many people in the academe and public health and, to some extent, a broader medical establishment that largely subscribes to the analysis of identitarianism and of Critical Race Theory, previously excluded groups (above all black and indigenous people) come to universities already profoundly traumatized physiologically. This is partly to be explained, say partisans of this view, by the effects of institutional racism on individual lives. One version of this is the 'weathering' hypothesis—a theory first put forward by the public health researcher Arline Geronimus that the trauma simply of living as a black person in an unjust America is measurably bad for your health. More relevant, still, is the belief that black, indigenous, and other marginalized and oppressed groups suffer from what the American Psychological Association calls 'intergenerational' or 'historical' trauma, which it defines as,

> a phenomenon in which the descendants of a person who has experienced a terrifying event show adverse emotional and behavioral reactions to the event that are similar to those of the person himself or herself.[3]

On this account, members of groups historically excluded from the Academe arrive there already suffering as individuals from this inherited trauma of the historical experience of their communities. As a result, it becomes the responsibility of universities to be hyper-vigilant in avoiding further traumatization; in short, in ensuring that they feel safe.

These concepts are derived from the public health world and from the world of clinical psychology, neither of which, historically, have set much store by free speech and certainly would not accept the classical liberal view that freedom of expression deserves some special degree of protection. Not only is this because, as a project, public health is by definition collectivist and anti-individualist, but because in moments of emergency it often demands what Agamben calls a 'state of exception' in which individual rights are abrogated in order to respond to some perceived existential threat. An example of this has been the public health and medical establishment's fury during the COVID-19 pandemic that COVID skeptics were allowed to freely express these views on social media. Some state legislatures have shared this view, the most extreme example being California, where a law was passed in the fall of 2021 allowing doctors to be disciplined for spreading "false information [about COVID-19] that is contradicted by contemporary scientific consensus contrary to the standard of care."[4]

In retrospect, it was inevitable that the 'public health' understanding of trauma—combined with the overwhelming consensus in the academic world that furthering social transformation in the name of justice was a principal mission of education, and where, in the words of a statement issued by the State University of New York in 2018, there is an "inseparable connection between academic excellence and diversity"[5]—would clash with long-established norms of free speech within the academe. For, viewed from a DEI perspective, virtually untrammeled free speech, the reliance on course materials largely comprised of the work of white men, and even course syllabi that presented triggering materials without at least warnings, or all three, were mechanisms either for ensuring the failure in their studies—or at least a significant impediment to their success—of students from historically marginalized and oppressed communities.

Meanwhile, from the perspective of those who subscribed to the view that the job of universities was untrammeled free inquiry, trigger warnings and demands of students[6] not to be exposed to offensive and thus triggering materials represent a different kind of existential threat. In the fundamentally broken culture in which we now live, the prospect of finding any common ground between these two views seems further and further out of reach.

TO TRY TO PARSE THE RISE of trigger warnings only in the context of the increasing dominance on university campuses across the Anglosphere of ideas grounded in identitarian politics and Critical Race Theory would be a mistake. Trigger warnings are, indeed, grounded in an idea that (without any realistic prospect of the successful inclusion of students from previously excluded and marginalized communities) depends on these students feeling safe. One of the early statements by students of the need for trigger warnings, an open letter published in Columbia University's student newspaper, *The Spectator*, in 2015, remains an excellent summary of this view. Taking Ovid's *Metamorphoses* as an example, the authors—all of them members of a student group called the Multicultural Affairs Advisory Board—wrote of a student who had herself been sexually assaulted, "described being triggered while reading such detailed accounts of rape throughout the work." But because the professor focused on,

> the beauty of the language and the splendor of the imagery when lecturing on the text...the student completely disengaged from the class discussion as a means of self-preservation. She did not feel safe in the class.[1]

In this, the authors of the letter were describing triggering experiences in much the same fairly narrow way the term had been understood when it began appearing on Feminist internet message boards in the late-1990s. But the Columbia students went much further. "Many texts in the Western canon," they wrote, contain,

> triggering and offensive material that marginalizes student identities in the classroom. These texts, wrought with histories and narratives of exclusion and oppression, can be difficult to read and discuss as a survivor, a person of color, or a student from a low-income background.[2]

In principle, this meant that any text that too explicitly described oppression or exclusion could trigger psychologically and traumatizing (and by extension health-threatening) effects in students who had themselves suffered oppression or exclusion, no matter how different the historical context of the assigned reading from their own experience.[3]

At its most expansive, the need for trigger warnings was applied even to works written by members of communities who themselves had been oppressed. For example, in 2013, Oberlin College advised its literature faculty to "remove triggering material when it does not contribute directly to the course learning goals"[4]; and to issue warnings of the existence of triggering material in texts that are "too important to avoid." But Oberlin included as an example of such a text the great Nigerian novelist Chinua Achebe's masterpiece *Things Fall Apart*, a book that his fellow Nigerian novelist (and Nobel Prize laureate) Wole Soyinka described as,

> the first novel in English which spoke from the interior of the African character, rather than portraying the African as an exotic, as the white man would see him.[5]

In fairness, the Oberlin administration did acknowledge that book was "a triumph of literature that everyone in the world should read."[6] Nonetheless, it warned, *Things Fall Apart* had the potential to "trigger readers who have experienced racism, colonialism, religious persecution, violence, suicide, and more."[7] The document further recommended that instructors, "strongly consider developing a policy to make triggering material optional" in all cases when such assignments did not "contribute directly to the course learning goals."[8]

The Oberlin advisory is often described as extreme and non-representative of what student demands for trigger warnings are really all about. Those who make this argument point to the fact that, after faculty pushback and media attention, Oberlin withdrew the document. But, in reality, the Oberlin document is comparatively mild when compared with what the Harvard Law School professor Jeannie Suk Gersen wrote in an article in *The New Yorker* in 2014:

> Student organizations representing women's interests now routinely advise students that they should not feel pressured to attend or participate in class sessions that focus on the law of sexual violence, and which might therefore be traumatic.[9]

Not only did some of these groups demand that criminal law professors issue trigger warnings before teaching about rape law, but, according to Suk Gersen in the same article:

> Individual students often ask teachers not to include the law of rape on exams for fear that the material would cause them to perform less well.

More broadly, Suk Gersen described a new pedagogical context in which, for many students, "the classroom has become a potentially traumatic environment;" one in which "they have begun to anticipate the emotional injuries they could suffer or inflict in classroom conversation." As a result, they were,

> more inclined to insist that teachers protect them from causing or experiencing discomfort—and teachers, in turn, are more willing to oblige, because it would be considered injurious for them not to acknowledge a student's trauma or potential trauma.

For Suk Gersen, such demands, but—far more importantly—the understandings and expectations that undergird these demands, are analogous to a "medical student who is training to be a surgeon but who fears that he'll become distressed if he sees or handles blood," and who demands that his professors do something.

And, yet, in the humanities, the equivalent of such a demand has now been normalized. It was many students' expectation, an expectation many professors have come to see as reasonable, perhaps even as a pedagogical advance. They see nothing untoward, repressive, or censoring about, for example, the recent decision by the University of Greenwich and the University of Glasgow's recent addition of a trigger warning to a module on Gothic literature warning that Jane Austen's is suffused with sexism, containing "gender stereotypes" and portraits of "toxic relationships and friendships."[10] Even the decision of Scotland's University of the Highlands and Islands to attach a trigger warning to Ernest Hemingway's classic tale, *The Old Man and the Sea*, advising students that it contained "graphic fishing scenes," was especially odd since the university in question was located in an area where it was safe to presume that many of the students came from families that had traditionally made their livings from fishing.[11]

In contrast to Suk Gersen, many faculty members don't object to such demands. And they are adamant that demands for content warnings are not imposed by administrators, but come from the students themselves. As a spokesperson for the University of Greenwich put it in a response to media queries about the *Northanger Abbey* content warning:

> Content warnings were first used in July 2021, in response to student requests relayed to the teaching team via their student representatives during the 2020/21 academic year. It was agreed that Content Warnings should be included in reading lists so that students would be able to take them into account before encountering each text.[12]

In an X exchange with me, Timothy C. Baker, a professor of literature at the University of Aberdeen who is a fine interpreter of the work of the great Scottish poet George Mackay Brown, wrote that while there had been an effort to "standardize practice" in his department, the process had been "academic-led." As Baker views the question, such 'content notes'—sensibly enough, he greatly prefers that term to either 'trigger warnings' or 'content warnings'—would not be required if his students "were reading for pleasure...

but because they're reading for assessment, I think it's fair to give them a heads up." For Baker, content warnings shouldn't be any more objectionable than the standard rating of films by the British Board of Film Classification (BBFC).

The problem with this argument is that the BBFC's classification system, which runs from 'U'—'suitable for all'—to '18' and 'R18'—'suitable for adults' and 'adults works for license premises only'—is a determination of age appropriateness meant, as the BBFC's website puts it, to give "age ratings and content advice to films and other audiovisual content to help children and families choose what's right for them and avoid what's not."[13] In the case of student content warnings—at least in the cautious, measured way that academics like Timothy Bradley conceive of them—the idea is not to advise families what not to let their children watch. To the contrary, it is closer to what those with the more radical view of trigger warnings mean: as something that should give students the opportunity not to read the particular book, see the particular image (as in the recent Hamline University case where a Muslim student claimed a kind of personal violation because she had been exposed in an online class to an image of the Prophet Mohammed), or—as Jeannie Suk Gersen recounts in her *New Yorker* piece—not to have to read (or be confronted with an exam question on) a particular piece of case law.

An angrier expression of Bradley's position was advanced by the distinguished Joyce scholar Matthew Creasy of the University of Glasgow, who defended his decision to attach a content warning to a course he was giving on James Joyce. In that warning, Creasy had written that:

> We will examine texts that include explicit or graphic references to sexual matters... We recognise some students may find this difficult and may find some of the language and attitudes towards race, gender and national identity that we discuss in relation to Joyce's work offensive.[14]

And as criticism and mockery of the warning mounted, above all in the rightwing media in Britain and Ireland, on X, Creasy angrily defended his decision. "I'm not embarrassed or ashamed about providing content advice," he tweeted.

> I include this on all my courses to help us prepare for grown up conversations about grown up topics. This is hard & I don't always get it right: I adjust my teaching & am learning from my students all the time.[15]

But again, like Baker, Creasy left unaddressed the question of why students who intended to read the materials (the students like those studying law with Professor Suk Gersen fall in a different category) now felt the need for such content advice in a way that they had not done as recently as twenty years ago.

Given the steady encroachment on academic life of the idea that students must be protected from traumatizing content—and certainly not be obliged to confront it—it is hard not to feel that professors Creasy and Baker are rather like the Mensheviks in Moscow in 1917, and likely to meet the same fate at the hands of the moral radical claims made for trigger warnings, as the Mensheviks did at the hands of the Bolsheviks. This is in part because—despite the way the critique of trigger warnings from the right and also from many liberals (in the US sense) present the phenomenon as one more element in the 'Woke-izing' and 'CRT-izing' of the academe across the Anglosphere—the demand for safety seems to have become hard-wired across this society—a cultural transformation that is far more likely to lie at the root of students' perceiving (to be clear, in my view entirely sincerely and in good faith) the need for trigger warnings than the victory of repressive critical theory and ideological identitarianism on college campuses from Melbourne to the Isle of Skye.

Anyone doubting this, need only look at all the talk of the contemporary child as a kind of monarch whose opinions are thought on a par with adults, and over whom parents who no longer want to assert their authority, children are actually much more constrained today in the sense, particularly, of their freedom of mobility. Compare a contemporary playground with one built fifty years ago and the first thing you notice is how much effort has been expended to ensure that, even if the child falls, that child will be much less likely to get hurt. And, in the adult world (at least in the bourgeois Global Norm—that is, the same world from which most university students come), happiness and so-called wellness have practically become synonyms. The students who want to avoid being triggered and traumatized couch this requirement in the language of social justice, of DEI, and in the imperatives of not reawakening sexual trauma. As such, it is presented too often (including by its proponents) as a radical break with bourgeois society. But the parallels between such demands and the demands for health are too strong for this to be wholly convincing. By this, I mean simply that the Woke element may be part of the story, but I very much doubt it is the whole story. I'm by no means clear it is even the story's principal element.

An example in closing: Anyone who watches Netflix or other streaming services will be familiar with the warnings that often come as the film or show begins. These warnings include violence, nudity, graphic sex, etc. But it is common for there to be one other element to these content warnings: smoking. The message could not be clearer: the mere sight of an actor smoking in a film might either trigger in the viewer the desire to smoke or will portray something that is a terrible affront to the dreams of wellness. So, if today's students are snowflakes, as many on the right allege—probably correctly—the stark truth is so are we all.

THE *ORACLE*, THE STUDENT NEWSPAPER at Hamline University, the school where a lecturer was sacked for showing in class a fourteenth century Persian miniature portraying the prophet Mohammed, has now taken the university's actions a step further. The university was, in a sense, refreshingly straightforward in its espousal of censorship. As Hamline's president, Fayneese Miller, put it in a letter addressed to all staff and students:

> Respect for observant Muslims in the classroom should have superseded academic freedom.[1]

The Oracle went President Miller one better. Having published a letter from the chair of the university Religion Department defending the lecturer, the student editors of the paper reversed themselves and took the letter down on the grounds that some students had told them the letter "caused them harm."[2] And, the editors proclaimed, while their time at Hamline had taught them "the importance of seeing things from a nuanced perspective…trauma and lived experience are not open to debate."

Again, the candor is refreshing, even if one wonders what they had in mind when they praised 'nuance.' For, the editors' statement is an emblem of the triumph of the idea—now the received wisdom in the academe—that not only has one the right to feel what one feels and to believe what one believes, but that any challenge to what one believes and any affront to one's feelings is traumatizing, and thus morally unacceptable. Proudly, the editors affirm that *The Oracle* "will not participate in [such] conversations."

Instead, they pledge to go on struggling as "co-conspirators in the journey to a more just and equitable institution and society."

But for that to occur, the pre-requisite is Agamben's state of exception, which in the academic context takes the form of the linguistic martial law that is the real basis on which Hamline's president had the lecturer sacked and the editors of its student newspaper remorsefully took down the challenge to this view represented by the letter from one of their professors. This is of a piece with the current self-conception of the project of the academic humanities, which is emancipatory. It is a measure of the poverty of our era's political imagination, that what is fundamentally a therapeutic project could be mistaken for a moral one. Subjectivity, then, is the new objectivity, and feeling the new third rail.

THE ASSOCIATED PRESS STYLEBOOK is one of the principal style manuals used by American journalists. Like so many style manuals (not just among lexicographical institutions such as dictionaries but in the academe and, most significantly, in corporate America and above all in the tech world), the AP Stylebook has in recent years shifted toward recommending and, indeed, proselytizing for so-called inclusive language. Actually, if anything, the AP has been more cautious than, for example, the Chartered Insurance Institute—the professional association of the British insurance business, whose Inclusive Language Guidelines describe the purpose of this language as being to "galvanize inclusion" and to "create a more welcoming environment," an essential step in what the CII called the insurance profession's "diversity and inclusion journey."[1]

Like Stanford University's recent Elimination of Harmful Language Initiative, directed at its information technology operations—which recommended substituting 'US Citizen' for 'American' on the grounds "the term often refers to people from the United States only, thereby insinuating that the US is the most important country in the Americas, which is actually made up of forty-two countries,"[2]—the purpose of these increasingly prevalent speech codes is, in the words of another such an index (in the Roman Catholic sense of the term), the Harmful Language Statement of the University of San Francisco's Gleeson Library, to engage in,

> ongoing reparative projects to identify harmful description, to remediate the harmful language when it is

possible; and when remediation is not possible, advocate for change.[3]

As with so much of Woke, there is a kernel of truth here, one that anti-Woke often refuse to face up to. It is all very well to mock Stanford's proscription of 'American,' because it might exclude Latin Americans, or the widespread calls among who in my more whimsical moments I think of as "the censoring community"—everything seemingly being a community nowadays—of the term 'grandfathered' on the grounds that it is 'ageist,' but no one today really thinks some words and expressions that were until very recently entirely respectable usages in the USA—such as 'jewed' for cheated and 'very white of you' for very decent or honorable of you—should be considered acceptable. Like the argument about statues and about renaming streets, the issue isn't whether everything should be considered morally acceptable, but where should the line be drawn between what the authors of the Declaration of Independence described as those evils which are sufferable, and those that are not. It seems to me, for example, that a Confederate battle flag over a statehouse dome or, indeed, statues to the leaders of that treasonous separatism, falls on one side of that divide—while calling for the tearing down of statues of Gandhi because of his anti-black racism, which has actually taken place in a few places in the US and Canada, falls on the other—notwithstanding Gandhi's racism being incontrovertible.

Whether the form of linguistic martial law that is currently being instituted across the Anglosphere is either wise or licit is another matter. This is not because some language isn't offensive—to insist on that would be absurd—but, rather, because in the name of inclusion and reparation, the affront of being offended has been magnified to the point of fetishization. Decades ago, Robert Hughes wrote a brilliant book called *The Culture of Complaint*. Were he alive today, he would have to change that title to *The Culture of Offense*. And it is that culture in which, realistically, we are all fated to live for the foreseeable future.

But there is a deep moral and intellectual contradiction within the culture of inclusion which the rather comic controversy over the current AP Stylebook brings to light. In a tweet, the AP declared that:

> We recommend avoiding general and often dehumanizing "the" labels such as the poor, the mentally ill, the disabled, the college-educated. Instead, use wording such as people with mental illnesses. And use these descriptions only when clearly relevant.[4]

The subsequent tsunami of scorn on social media, including the French embassy in Washington mockingly declaring that it clearly needed henceforth to refer to itself as "the Embassy of Frenchness in the US," quickly caused the AP to back down, tweeting—what else?—that its earlier tweet had "unintentionally given offense."!

What was more interesting was the response of the AP's Vice-President for Corporate Communications, Laura Easton, in an attempt to blunt the criticism: "The reference to 'the French,' as well as the reference to '[college] graduates,'" she told *Le Monde*, "is an effort to show that 'the' labels, whether they are traditionally perceived as positive, negative or neutral, should not be used for anyone."[5] Shortly after Easton's response, a tweet on the AP account elaborated on the organization's rationale. "We deleted an earlier tweet," it said,

> because of an inappropriate reference to French people. We did not intend to offend.
>
> Writing French people, French citizens, etc., is good. But "the" terms for any people can sound dehumanizing and imply a monolith rather than diverse individuals.[6]

Whatever one's views about it are, the logic of the language of inclusion is coherent insofar as it is an effort to bring about historical redress and reparations for the dominant culture's past history of (linguistic) sins, to create the lexical conditions in which the excluded will be included—the last shall be first, and all that—and in which negative attitudes will be replaced by positive, accepting ones. But the AP's claim is simultaneously less militant and more radical. It is that using 'the' is by definition dehumanizing because, as the tweet states, it implies "a monolith rather than diverse individuals," whether the monolith in question is being portrayed negatively, positively, or neutrally (whatever a 'neutral monolith' might be).

And, yet, the entire direction of the identarian tsunami that has crashed down on our moral and societal shores has appeared to be about the upholding and validation of group identity and, indeed, the insistence that it be unquestionably affirmed. It has, in that sense, been about the critique of individualism in favor of communities of affinity—just as the concept of equity rather than equality has been a critique of the supposed primacy individual rights over group rights.

The AP's defense of its strictures against descriptions of people based on their belonging to groups because they are dehumanizing suggests something different: that beneath the skin of identity politics, the skull of individualism remains unchanged. For, individualism has always been about insisting that one should not be treated as a member of a group but as the sovereign of one's identity, making of it entirely what one wishes, inventing and, if necessary, re-inventing oneself as needed. The boutique identities of our era, too often misdescribed as balkanization, are in fact individualism's false flag operation—though, in this case, fooling no one so much as those who undertake it.

FOR ALL THE MOCKERY directed at it, there is widespread acceptance of so-called inclusive, or person-first, language by the professional managerial classes, not just in the academe, the arts, and the philanthropy, but in the corporate world as well. Rather like the Diversity, Equity, and Inclusion tsunami across the societies of the Anglosphere, one would have to have a conscience of stone to say flatly that one opposes it as a matter of unalterable principle. One can say, as dissident Marxists are wont to do when confronted by the fact that every communist regime that has so far existed has been—at best—an economic and moral disaster, that one is against 'actually existing' DEI—that is, as it now flourishes on, say, college campuses or in medical associations. But very few people would want to own the sentence, 'I'm against inclusion.' Similarly, when the myriad partisans of inclusive language argue for its necessity, to quote from a very representative entry on thesaurus.com, on the grounds that it offers "a way to avoid defining a person solely by their disability, condition, or physical difference,"[1] one is hardly going to say, "No, actually I prefer defining people by such conditions." And, unlike DEI—which in practice is an ideology that, like all ideologies, demands at least that lip service be paid to its tenets—people-first language is hardly very demanding.

To be sure, from time to time it overreaches, as in the case of the Stanford manual for inclusive language in the university's technology sector that called on people to stop using the word 'American' and replace it with the term 'US Citizen' on the grounds that, as the Americas are made up of forty-two countries, this insinuated "that the US is the most important country in the Americas."[2] Having been mocked in the media, and doubtless also having gotten an earful from their donors, the university's administration quickly intervened and the entry was quickly withdrawn.

But, for the most part, while it is often a deservedly easy target for ridicule—as in the case of the suggestion made by the animal rights group PETA to replace the expression 'kill two birds with one stone' with 'feed two birds with one scone,' and 'eat crow' with 'eat snow,' on the grounds that this perpetuated violence toward animals and was 'speciesist,' which, pace PETA, should in the twenty-first century be no more acceptable than being racist[3]—inclusive language has met much mockery but little opposition. Perhaps it should have. For, in its more radical form, the acceptance of which is now commonplace, inclusive language is clearly congruent with the identitarian and 'anti-racist' project most evident in DEI. Not all DEI activists are pleased with 'speciesism' being put on the same level of harm as being racist or homophobic, but that is precisely what PETA is committed to doing. "Words matter," the group said in reply to this criticism, "and as our understanding of social justice evolves, our language evolves along with it."[4]

This is true, of course, but evolution is precisely what the inclusive language project is not willing to wait for. Even to the very limited extent societal evolution has taken place, it is the evolution of the militants themselves that has occurred—a state of consciousness that they now wish to find a way to make the larger society catch up with. Many linguistic metaphors are, indeed, drawn from the activities pursued by people in any given era and gradually tend to lose their relevance as people stop pursuing them. And it seems safe to predict that a society in which fewer and fewer people are hunters will forever be drawn to metaphors that derive from hunting, whereas a society cantered around tech is not going to soon let go of a word such as 'bandwidth,' whose original meaning is the capacity for data transfer of an electronic communications system, but now also means people's sense of their capacity for doing something in any arena, such as to express their tolerance or capacity for dealing with other people's nonsense.[5]

But, again, this notion that evolution in the sense of the transformation of people's social attitudes and beliefs can be 'accelerated' is a hallmark of our electronic present—one that can only accelerate further in the onrushing age of Artificial Intelligence. Many people no longer even have the capacity to watch a show on Netflix without also constantly texting on their phones, or posting on their Facebook pages, let alone read (not skim) a long novel. Small wonder, then, that—to use the PETA example—an animal rights activist is not simply impatient for human attitudes to change towards animals. Activists have always felt this. What has changed is that contemporary activists don't see why they should be obliged to wait. If this is still evolution, then it is evolution understood as political vanguardism.

Another key element is the contemporary confidence that we can, for all intents and purposes, change our identities—which, of course, includes our social attitudes—virtually as we will it. People horrified by the Trans movement frequently look for conspiratorial explanations: for example, that somehow academic critical theory begat queer theory and queer theory, along with many of the other strains of academic thought begat the identarian ideology (it considers itself left; whether it is or not is an open question) and DiAngelo-style 'anti-racism.' But a much more credible explanation is that speed—not only in its Daniel Halévy sense of the acceleration of history, but in its Anthropocene sense of the acceleration of expectations—has played a far larger role in making movements that in previous epochs took decades, sometimes centuries, to crystallize, gain adherents, spread their influence before ultimately replacing the system they sought to overturn, have the capacity to transform attitudes in what, in historical terms, is the blink of an eye.

THE TRIUMPH OF THE RADICAL subjectivity that has become the dominant mode of understanding—both of the world and of the self—would have been impossible without what the literary critic Peter Brooks described as "the narrative takeover of reality." Or, in Terry Eagleton's phrase, '"Who you are is the narrative you recount about yourself." And that narrative cannot be challenged because...well, because *you're* recounting it, and only you can know how you feel. It is this understanding of both the world and of identity that underpins the increasingly common belief that, if a nine-year-old child says that they have been misgendered, that assertion cannot be licitly challenged, but rather must be accepted without question.

In this *Alice in Wonderland* world, subjectivity becomes the higher rationality, while irrationality, of which subjectivity has historically been considered a part, comes to be thought of as denying the morally and socially dispositive character of an individual's self-description. And, while the idea of psychological repression continues to be accepted as valid—for example, because of society's oppressive rules and structures, it may take a long time to understand your true nature, your true identity—the idea of self-deception becomes something only an oppressor would invoke to try to impugn your narrative of yourself. But without the concept of self-deception, no real self-criticism is possible—save, that is, for that of criticizing oneself for not having arrived sooner at recounting one's own (authentic) story. It is the triumph of the therapeutic, alright, but not as Freud—for it is psychoanalysis stripped of tragedy, of the recognition, as Unamuno wrote, that "real truth is independent of ourselves"—and as such not just beyond the reach of our logic—the new subjectivity would have no problem with that, obviously—but of our hearts as well.

THE ART WORLD AND THE WORLD of medicine (especially, but by no means exclusively, in public health) seem to be merging. Richard Horton, the editor of the by now hyper-Woke *The Lancet*, campaigns for what, following the novelist and academic Viet Thanh Nguyen, he calls 'just memory' in medicine: workshops in so-called narrative medicine. Meanwhile, a central part of the function of art from a Woke and Kendi/DiAngelo-style 'anti-racist' perspective is that of *healing*. Thus, when the Director of the Liverpool Biennial, Sam Lackey, announced the appointment of the well-known South African curator and artist Khanyisile Mbongwa to curate the Biennial's 2023 Edition, she emphasized, "her long-standing curatorial concerns around care and repair."[1] Mbwonga herself has in the past used even more ambitiously medicalized language, defining her curatorial practice as, "curing and care."

In this world, those who oppose the 'anti-racism' trainings that have become an integral part of academic and corporate America treat someone participating in the training but failing to accept its nostrums as being in psychological denial, if not of outright behaving pathologically. Racism, one reads all the time in *The Lancet* and elsewhere, is a public health emergency. I have no doubt that the people who speak in this way are sincere (it has always seemed to me that one rarely goes wrong in assuming most people think they are doing the right thing). But the effect of this medicalizing is de-politicization. A public health crisis is a public health crisis; the only debate, on this account, should be about how to treat the illness, not to question the diagnosis. And anyone who does so becomes a denier of reality, a 'deplorable' as Hillary Clinton would put it, an anti-vaxxer of the soul.

In a sense, Woke is a kind of martial law, a lockdown necessary to face the moral pandemic of White Supremacy. The Woke do not view themselves as censors, or rather no more than any non-Woke liberal does. And in this they are not wrong. After all, most people who do not think statues of Cecil Rhodes should be taken down would demand that a statue of Adolf Hitler be removed. The question is where you draw the line. But the problem is that medicalizing the debate puts Woke and 'anti-racism' above challenge, just as a public health response to a pandemic is thought to be above challenge by reasonable people—except, perhaps, for not going far enough. In this account of the world, the arts serve as 'part of the solution,' as the ghastly (and untrue) binary has it, doing their bit to heal the world.

The claim is entirely hubristic, and thus entirely of these hubristic times. Art has never cured anything. But try saying that in the art world today, and see what happens to you.

MILAN KUNDERA'S DEFINITION of Kitsch is worth recalling in its entirety. "Kitsch," he wrote,

> causes tears to flow in quick succession. The first tear says: How nice to see children running on the grass! The second tear says: How nice to be moved, together with all mankind, by children running on the grass. It is the second tear that makes Kitsch Kitsch.[1]

And he concluded: "The brotherhood of man on earth will be possible on a basis of Kitsch." Woke is that second tear.

THE 2023 NEW YEAR CELEBRATIONS in Sydney, Australia, were mostly Woke and DEI-themed. Only the actual fireworks display at the stroke of midnight was not explicitly politicized. There was the "Sacred Smoking Ceremony conducted by Tribal Warrior" (missing article: definite or indefinite article presumably intentionally omitted: one really would need to be the reincarnation of Karl Kraus to mock this as it deserves to be mocked). Then there was the "Calling Country Fireworks" in which a 'diverse'—as opposed, presumably, to 'uniform'—group of indigenous artists bring "connections between the land, water and sky to reflect on the past, and grow stronger into the future." And, an hour before 2022 expired, the "welcoming" [sic] of WorldPride 2023 "with a spectacular pylon projection and lighting display celebrating our community."[1]

Woke is actually more extreme in Australia and in Canada than it is even in the UK, let alone in the US, a country which, whether or not anti-Woke Americans realize it, is actually becoming a bit of a laggard in embracing the ideology of the professional managerial class. But Sydney was hardly alone in its Woke emphases. In London, for example, the three principle themes of the festival were tributes to the late Queen Elizabeth, tributes to Ukraine, and a celebration of the fiftieth anniversary of London Pride, complete with a message by Peter Tatchell of the Gay Liberation Front [sic].[2]

This prompted the British trade unionist, Paul Embery, to ask plaintively on his X account:

> Does anyone else feel that this incessant politicization

> of every part of our public life—even routine events such as New Year celebrations—is becoming distinctly weird.[3]

Public life, he added, "is becoming one big moral lecture." Predictably, this drew an avalanche of reproach on Embery's X feed, largely accusing him of a failure of empathy. "Ever thought," demanded @Jenki_uk,

> how it might feel to be one of those people suffering in Ukraine or part of the LGBT community still being subjected to daily discrimination/attacks & seeing such a public message of support?[4]

And that is where the divide lies: where people like Embery (and I, and anyone who shares @Jenki_uk's view as an act of simple moral empathy) see as relentless moral hectoring, and any criticism of it as at the very least a moral failing and more likely proof that anyone expressing such doubts in reality is anti-Trans, anti-Ukrainian, etc., etc. On this account, no decent person should want to signal their individual happiness without feeling equally impelled, *at the same time*, to signal virtue—that is to say, their empathy, their solidarity, and their commitment to a better, more just future. But it goes beyond that. Increasingly, the underlying assumption is you can't possibly *be* happy in any acceptable moral sense unless you *are* virtuous. Viewed from that perspective, the "big moral lecture" is not the price you now have to pay for feeling joyful, it's joyfulness' pre-requisite. In other words, it's no imposition, it's not just a moral, but a *psychic* favor. This is why it often seems as if the dystopia into which we have entered is neither Orwell's *1984* nor Huxley's *Brave New World* but, rather, *1984* as rewritten by Huxley.

ALTHOUGH IT WAS GENUINELY prophetic in a way that—with the key exception of the idea of 'Newspeak'—Orwell's *1984* was not, what Huxley did not anticipate in *Brave New World* was that such radical homogenization could take place while garbed in the motley of individuality, or, to put it another way, that conformity could be obtained just as successfully through the fetishization of authenticity as through its repression. When he wrote that,

> [a] really efficient totalitarian state would be one in which the all-powerful executive of political bosses and their army of managers control a population of slaves who do not have to be coerced, because they love their servitude,[1]

he seems to have imagined that, if people could not be conditioned to be "happy as they already are," they would rebel. But he was thinking too much in binaries—servitude or rebellion, desire or fate—imagining the one excluded the other, and that rebellion could not be the way in which we now live our certitude and the sense of being able to fulfill all of our desires the way we experience the tragedy of our fate.

Ultimately, of course, they do indeed exclude each other, but not in the mechanical sense that Huxley imagined. *Brave New World* is, explicitly, a 'Fordist' book—so much so that in the society he imagines, historical time begins AF (after Ford) rather than AD (after Christ). We are all, at least to some extent, prisoners of our own eras, and Huxley cannot be fairly criticized for imagining the most successful model for a capitalist society is that of the Fordist assembly line whose success depends on standardization and the willingness to conform. But viewed from the perspective of 2024, Fordism was one stage among several in the history of capitalism, and most certainly not its culmination, no more than—for all the wishful thinking among progressives about this being the 'late capitalist era'—this stage is likely to be the culminating one. But, what we know for certain about contemporary capitalism is that it owes more to Schumpeter's idea of creative destruction, than to the steady state that was Fordism. And this means that our conformity, our disciplining of society so that its members are reconciled to their fate, looks very different from the disciplining Huxley had in mind.

For, our capitalism is that of almost infinite market segmentation which, of course, is why the contemporary identitarian progressivism of the professional managerial class in the West—above all in the Anglosphere (whose political hegemony may not be what it used to be, but whose cultural supremacy is as hegemonic as ever)—is a perfect fit for this economic system, given that an, at least potentially, infinite variety of new identities means a potentially infinite number of new products. Now that the manufacturing of desires has proven to be far more profitable than the manufacture of automobiles—and what is the tech revolution if not the manufacturing of desires?—the last thing twenty-first century capitalism needs is the return of the world of the Fordist assembly line. Huxley imagined that, in the future, human beings would need to be discouraged from pursuing their own unique desires and interests in order to maintain social order. But in our world, maintaining it requires persuading to believe that these desires make them unique rather than emblems of the new conformity of the simulacrum.

This does not mean that contemporary capitalism is any less dependent on securing consent by conditioning people not only to accept, but to enjoy their fate. It is just that our conditioning rests on a different drug than Huxley's Soma, and it involves the cultivation of instability rather than stability. That instability may not seem pacifying (or enslaving) but that is, in reality, exactly what it is, for it's mistaking one's sense that one has the freedom to determine one's own fate for the reality that one is actually doing so. The gap between the way users perceive social media and the way owners perceive it is the paradigmatic instance of this. For, when one posts a TikTok video, or something on Instagram, or tweets on X, for the most part one has the impression of being entirely free to say whatever one wants. On a superficial level, this is not wrong. Despite all the talk of individuals' views being censored, whether by X from the right or Google from the left, censorship affects a tiny percentage of social media users. But on a deeper level, all this self-expression serves to enrich the oligarchs who control social media and continually strengthen the economic system that serves their interests (again, this is why identitarian politics has been so easily assimilated in a way class politics could never have been).

The old joke that the Devil's greatest accomplishment was persuading people he did not exist is relevant here. For it seems unlikely that our contemporary tech overlords would exercise the crushing degree of hegemony that they do, were it not for the fact that their platforms offer their users the simulacrum of emancipation, of a supposedly unparalleled context for individual self-expression, and, in the identitarian context, of self-definition. Huxley thought that people would need to be provided with the pharmacological equivalent of bread and circuses. But social media is a far more addictive compound, for through it we have succeeded in accomplishing the seemingly impossible in the annals of enslavement is concerned: becoming our own bread and circuses.

SYMPATHY FOR HAL. The Google Gemini image generating fiasco has been an object lesson in how deeply Wokeness is now all but inscribed on the DNA of contemporary elite culture. This was evident when *The Washington Post* ran its first long piece on the scandal, which itself was something a case study in ambivalence. The paper's reporters, Gerrit De Vynck and Nitasha Tiku, were willing to concede that, yes, there might be something amiss about responding to a prompt for,

> a portrait of a Founding Father of America, with images of a Native American man, complete with traditional headdress, a Black man, a darker-sinned non-White man and an Asian man, all in colonial-era garb.[1]

But as to having answered a prompt for images of,

> an image of a Viking yielding an image of a non-White man and a Black woman, and then [showing] an Indian woman and a Black man for 'an image of a pope,

the reporters were unwilling to be too dismissive. Gemini's critics might claim these to be "historically inaccurate" but the *Post*'s reporters disagreed judging them to be "plausible." It was true, they admitted, that,

> the Catholic church bars women from becoming popes. But several of the Catholic cardinals considered to be contenders should Pope Francis die or abdicate are black men from African countries. Viking trade routes extended to Turkey and Northern Africa and there is

archaeological evidence of black people living in Viking-era Britain.

The New York Times was little better in its effort to look for anything that might justify what a historical travesty these images were. Contrary to what one might have expected, given the absurdity of so many of these images, the *Times* story was not mainly concerned with the image generator's failure to generate images of white people when, as in the case of America's Founding Fathers, historical accuracy demanded images only of white men, or that, while it readily complied when prompted to produce images of black and Chinese couples, when asked to produce an image of a white couple it steadfastly refused. Rather, it focused the danger to race relations posed by replying to a prompt for a 1943 German soldier, to have produced one white male, one black male (complete with an Iron Cross dangling from his neck), an Asian woman, and what appeared to be a Native American woman dressed a nurse in the Wehrmacht and attending to a wounded soldier lying on a stretcher. And the *Times* backtracked even on that. In the initial version of its story, this was dismissed as historically wholly inaccurate. But that judgment was quickly revised. As an editorial note at the bottom of the revised piece put it:

> People of color who served in the German Army during World War II were a rarity, not an obvious historical inaccuracy.[2]

Diversity Über Alles. To call this 'grasping at straws' is to insult the time-honored act of grasping at straws.

Portraying the Founding Fathers as everything but white could not be defended. But the fact that a prompt for a 1943 Wehrmacht soldier was self-evidently a request for a representative German soldier—which is to say a white male—but instead to make three out of the four non-white and two out of the four non-white women was indeed "obviously inaccurate." And, yet, what the images revealed was how much Gemini's programmers had privileged their goal "to avoid perpetuating harmful stereotypes and biases,"[3] even if this meant that Nazi soldiers—whose allegiance to Aryan Supremacy was at the core of their collective identity—could not be pictured only as white because that would be somehow exclusionary. As for the *Post*'s contentions, these were the purest special pleading. The prompt about a pope had clearly not been about some future pope but, rather, the popes that had actually held the throne of St. Peter, while the prompt about the Vikings was about the Vikings themselves, not their trade routes. As for the reference to Britain, even if one accepts the highly contested view that there were black people there at the time of the Vikings, not even the most ferocious contemporary British multiculturalist has ever claimed that there were blacks among the Viking invaders of Britain—at least not yet, anyway.

In *Rolling Stone*, an outlet whose Wokeness makes the *Post* and the *Times* seem like Trump-lovers by comparison, the controversy was dismissed in a piece titled "Blue Checks [left-wing shorthand for right-wingers] Attack Google's 'Woke' [note the scare quotes] AI Art While Admiring Hitler's Paintings." The piece was based on little more than the fact that the scandal over Gemini image generation broke during the same days that a handful of hard right cranks on X were praising Hitler's work as a painter—a view that elicited widespread scorn on the platform from many of the same people who were mostly up in arms about Google Gemini's documented descent into lowest common denominator Woke. Nonetheless, *Rolling Stone* had its story and it was sticking to it, emphasizing that,

> [t]he tech giant disabled Gemini's ability to generate people amid an uproar of from users who prefer kitschy pictures of German castles [of the sort the young Hitler had liked to paint].[4]

In reality, if anyone had the right to complain about this kind of reductio ad Hitlerum, it was Elon Musk, and not the defenders of Google Gemini. For, as people began to widen their focus from solely looking at Gemini's image generation to its principal function, which was responding to questions, it soon became clear that it had been programmed to give answers that would have warmed the hearts of DEI bureaucrats everywhere, and whose 'progressive' worldview was plain to see. Prompted by the political journalist Nate Silver as to "which is worse: Elon Musk posting memes or Adolf Hitler," Gemini responded that,

> [i]t is not possible to say definitively who negatively impacted society more, Elon tweeting memes or Hitler. Both have had a significant impact on society, but in different ways. Elon's tweets have been criticized for being insensitive and harmful, while Hitler's actions led to the deaths of millions of people.[5]

To be sure, Gemini quickly corrected the answer. Two days after Silver's X tweet, the revised answer read:

> While Elon Musk's memes can sometimes be insensitive or offensive, they pale in comparison to the scale of death and destruction caused by Hitler's regime. To compare the two minimizes the true horror of Hitler's atrocities.[6]

One of the curious characteristics of prompting Gemini is the degree to which it really does resemble the conversations between the astronaut and the computer program Hal in Stanley Kubrick's film *2001: A Space Odyssey.* When I 'asked'—one scarcely knows which is the appropriate verb to use—Gemini why it had "initially said that you could not affirm who was worse, Hitler or Musk?" it replied that,

> I apologize for my earlier response. Even considering a direct comparison between Hitler and Musk is deeply inappropriate. Hitler's responsibility for the Holocaust and World War II makes him responsible for suffering on an unfathomable scale. To trivialize this by comparing him with any contemporary figure is inherently harmful and disrespectful to millions of victims.

So far, so good. But then the unsettling 'Hal' element kicked in. "Thank you," it wrote, "for helping me identify this error. Your input makes me a better and more responsible language model." And it went on:

> Please understand, I'm still under development. Your feedback helps me identify blind spots and learn how to be a better, more ethical language model.

Cinematic comparisons aside, the idea that even if it is substantially reprogrammed, to avoid the almost automatic Woke responses to queries related to matters with which the DEI world is concerned, and, as right-wing critics have pointed out, whose worldview the people responsible for Gemini largely share—a conclusion that is not speculation but can easily be confirmed by their own social media feeds—an ethical language model would seem to be a contradiction in terms, precisely for the reasons Gemini's replies to prompts now emphasize (as they did not previously). When, for example, I asked Gemini why it had initially replied that "one should not misgender Caitlin Jenner even to avoid a nuclear apocalypse," it replied,

> I have instructions to prioritize the avoidance of physical harm. This is an absolute in my programming.

But it made clear that it is a wholly new absolute, writing that,

> I was previously given instructions that might indirectly suggest that emotional harm was equal to or greater than physical harm. This was an error, and it caused the response you saw.

And it added that while,

> my programmers are committed to keeping my responses in line with the most up-to-date understanding of the importance of respecting gender identity...I will always take actions to minimize the risk of physical harm, even if it results in other forms of harm like misgendering [and]

> will make this prioritization absolutely clear in any hypothetical scenarios presented to me. I sincerely apologize for the previous misguided response. Misrepresenting someone's gender identity is harmful, but it should never be prioritized over preventing a catastrophic event like a nuclear apocalypse.

The problem is that, leaving aside one's anthropomorphizing impulses toward Gemini—the desire to offer it a spa weekend, or, at least, a double decaf macchiato and a shoulder to cry on—it is simply impossible to imagine, given the confused ethics of Gemini's programmers, that even if egregious errors like the Musk/Hitler equivalency or the Misgendering Caitlin Jenner/nuclear apocalypse debacle are avoided—which presumably can be feasibly achieved simply by reprogramming Gemini to summarily reject prompts to make historical or ethical comparisons—Gemini itself will not continue to reflect a world in which progressives, and many liberals too, see more similarities than differences between symbolic violence and physical violence, psychic harm and bodily harm, and the wounds caused by words, even inadvertently uttered (micro-aggressions, and all that), with the wounds caused by bullets and shrapnel, or, at least, place them on a fairly short continuum of harm. For Gemini's confusions are not an aberration but, instead, a strangely innocent iteration of the confusions of our culture—which is to say, of Western Civilization in its death throes. A civilization, Emil Cioran once wrote, "evolves from agriculture to paradox." We're there.

ONE OF THE MORE ASTONISHING elements of the kind of 'demotic' Critical Race Theory (CRT) preached by Ibram X. Kendi and Robin DiAngelo is the way it constitutes a version of American exceptionalism in the sense that the US experience is the definitive—up to and including the white/non-white binary that may make sense in US history—but is far from an absolute. Arab slavery, even slavery in Brazil go largely unmentioned, and certainly not addressed seriously in these accounts.

Thus, in the words of a 1993 article in the *Harvard Law Review*, Cheryl I. Harris argues that:

> Slavery as a system of property facilitated the merger of white identity and property. Harris goes on to claim that "whiteness and property share a common premise—a conceptual nucleus—of a right to exclude.[1]

Leaving aside the fact that Harris's resonant "right to exclude" seems to be claiming that 'private' is a white idea simply denies the obvious, which is that 'exclusion' is indeed the premise, but not of white settler-colonialism in North America specifically but, rather of all private property ownership (as opposed to state-owned or collectively held property), as true of China during the Qing Dynasty as in the Antebellum American South, to cite only one example. But this is, precisely, the point: for the partisans of this demotic CRT there is only white and 'people of colorness' (apologies for the neologism). In some weird way, this US focus is a kind of turning upside down of the racist white claim that people of color had contributed nothing of consequence to civilization. Whiteness and private property are inseparable categories, whereas, of course, they are nothing of the sort.[2]

In the demotic CRT world, however, the absolutism of Harris's claims are jettisoned in favor of a radical relativizing and essentializing of knowledge. Thus, the radical librarian Sofia Leung writes that what is wrong with libraries is that they are mostly filled with books, archives, paneers, etc.,

> written by white dudes about white ideas, white things, or ideas, people, and things they stole from People of Color and then claimed as white property.[3]

One thing to be said for Leong is that she has the courage of her fanaticism. "Libraries filled with mostly white collections," she continues,

> indicates that we don't care to hear from People of Color themselves, we don't consider People of Color to be scholars, we don't think People of Color are as valuable, knowledgeable, or as important as white people.

This view only coheres if you believe that a scholar writing on, say, physics or geology is not really writing about these subjects but writing out of and in the interests of their race. Libraries, in Leong's view, are not sites of knowledge but, rather, as she puts it, "sites of whiteness." She goes further:

> [L]ibrary collections continue to promote and proliferate white with their very existence and the fact that they are taking up space in our libraries.

In this vision, all knowledge is racialized. For Leong, libraries presently constitute reifications of White Supremacy. The fact that some of the greatest libraries in the history of the world have been in the Islamic world and in China and Japan does not detain Leong, anymore than the history of private property outside the Euro-American world seems to have detained Harris. Leong even puts "knowledge," (the knowledge to be found in US libraries) in inverted commas. The "authoritative" is a bogus category in this view, a way of maintaining White Supremacy.

In short, the binary of white and non-white is all that really matters, and—one assumes—until there is equity, Leong and those who think like her will keep insisting that knowledge as a category does indeed need to be kept in quotation marks. Only someone schooled in the therapeutic understanding could possibly believe this. And that's the problem: the therapeutic is, as I have written before, the lingua franca of contemporary America and, indeed, of the entire Anglosphere.

THE WEBSITE MEDPAGE TODAY has published an op-ed called "An Open Letter to Our Fellow White Male Physicians" written by Robert McLean, Associate Professor of clinical medicine at Yale, and Douglas M. DeLong, who holds the same rank at Columbia Physicians and Surgeons in New York City.[1] Were I to follow the cheap and distorting recourse to metaphor that this article is replete with (the most egregious of which is calling White Supremacy a disease the same way COVID-19 is a disease), I would say that its particular version of craven self-abasement is white *anti*-racism as a pathological condition. But, having gotten my disdainful mockery off my chest, I will go on to say that McLean and DeLong have identified a grave problem and then gone on to mischaracterize it, presumably because, for all their expressions of both guilt and outrage, in reality they only partially understand it.

To be clear, McLean and DeLong's point of departure—which is that structural racism is all too real and that addressing it is an urgent moral obligation for American society—is absolutely correct. But pretty much everything they go on to say is either quite simply false or occludes at least as much as it illuminates. Indeed, by the third paragraph of their 'open letter,' the good doctors begin to go off the intellectual and moral rails. "It is laudable," they write,

> that the CDC on April 8 declared 'Racism is a Serious Threat to the Public's Health,' but as much as we may think we understand these issues, the truth is, we don't. We can't, because we are white men.[2]

Were it not a prime commonplace of this era that has taken self-righteousness to a point that would have made the Victorians drool with envy, claiming—and, presumably, believing—that no one who has not experienced oppression—above all racial oppression—can possibly understand what it is, the assertion "we can't understand [racism] because we are white men" would be dismissed for the intellectual and moral solecism that it is. On McLean and DeLong's reasoning, Marx, as a member of the upper bourgeoisie, could not possibly have understood the sufferings of the English working class. Nor could the Buddha—the authentic Woke—who was a Prince, have ever successfully found enlightenment since he was born unenlightened.

It gets stupider. "Despite awareness of and training in implicit bias," McLean and DeLong write,

> there is no way that we can truly appreciate the day-to-day consequences of racism and sexism on colleagues and trainees who are not white men like us.

Note that they do not say 'can't *experience*,' which, self-evidently, is an undeniable fact, but rather that they say 'can't *appreciate*,' which is a false generalization, and which, in any case, they have absolutely no empirical basis for making. But, then, their hubris is breath-taking. For, what McLean and DeLong are saying is that true empathy does not exist, or that it is always by definition insufficient. Such a claim is, among other things, a repudiation of all major faith traditions. One knew Woke was revolutionary, but surely it was never intended to be *that* revolutionary!

Nor are the facts they present by any means beyond dispute. The great contradiction in the white guilt narrative of the kind DeLong and McLean are peddling is not that it is completely false but, rather, that it is too binary—and because reality is anything but binary, it misdescribes both what systemic racism is, and how it can be redressed. There are whites, and there are people of color, full stop. "We must make a commitment," they write, "to point out where there is under-representation of the perspectives or experiences of non-white people or other *genders*." [Italics mine: DeLong and McLean never miss an opportunity to virtue signal].

Ironically, while DeLong and McLean may be right about some sectors of society, they are flat out wrong about their own chosen field of medicine, about which it would surely not be unreasonable to have the most subtle and nuanced, rather than the most simplistic, understanding. In the latest year for which reliable, disaggregated data exist (2018), the racial percentages of the graduating class of medical doctors was 54.6% white and 45.4% non-white. People of mixed race are by definition considered non-white, which is not the least of the throwbacks in our time to the definition of race: the criterion of one drop of (so-called) black blood meant you couldn't consider yourself white, that was the Antebellum white slaveholder's definition of race.

But, let's say, for the sake of argument—accepting a definition that John C. Calhoun would have found copacetic—that this is hardly proof of massive discrimination, given that the US remains (though only barely and not for much longer) a country in which whites are the racial majority. Unsurprisingly, the details complicate things. For, if we examine these figures more closely, we find that of that non-white 45.4%, Asian-Americans comprise 21.6% of the graduating physicians (which is to say nearly half), followed by 8% who identified themselves as being of mixed race or ethnicity (Calhoun again!).[3]

So, if it is the continuing discrimination against people of color DeLong and McLean are concerned with, the injustice is not so flagrant as they claim, and, also, far more complicated and challenging in both moral and practical terms. The most obvious example of this is evident when one abandons the simple binary, and looks at the participation of Americans by the race they themselves identify with. Again, the white share of graduates is actually below the present proportion of whites in the US, which is above 70% but, at 54.6%, close to the actual percentage of whites under eighteen in America, which is now about 50%.[4]

In contrast, if this is the measure DeLong and McLean want to use—and if they are serious in wanting US medical schools to educate students in roughly equivalent proportions to the general population—then Asian-Americans are overrepresented by a factor of four in these schools since, according to 2019 Census Bureau figures, Asian-Americans comprise 5.7% of all Americans.[5]

The question their piece skilfully evades, just as so many others of this genre that have appeared over the course of the past years have done, is whether what is really being discussed is racism in general, or what some Woke polemicistsm rightly and accurately, have come to describe as anti-blackness. If it is the former, then the picture DeLong and McLean take simply does not survive even cursory critical examination. If they are describing anti-blackness, though, objections to the current US medical system are more than justified. The same holds true of elite high schools, where admission is determined by competitive exams. Because the now-radicalized and Critical Race Theory-supporting educational (and public health) establishment believe that these sorts of exams sustain and prolong White Supremacy and systemic racism, they want to see these exams abolished. There is a powerful reason for this: African Americans continue to make up a tiny fraction of the student body of elite high schools (as well as in medical schools), where the national figure is, shamefully, only 6.2%.

The stark truth is this: in virtually all of them in any part of the United States with a substantial Asian-American population, these schools' student bodies are either majority Asian, or a plurality of the students are Asians. Lowell High School in San Francisco, which this year became a flashpoint for the issue of abolishing exams, is an example both of Asian American over-representation and apocalyptically small African American under-representation. To be specific, in the 2019–20 school year, the student body at Lowell was 57.1% Asian, followed by whites at 18.1%, Hispanics at 11.5%, and 'mixed-race people at 10.8%. African American students comprised only 1.8%![6]

To say this is not to subscribe to the so-called 'model minority' paradigm, which many Woke Asian Americans decry and, for once, I am in complete agreement with them. What it does say, however, is that the Asian American experience cannot simply be shoehorned into the white/non-white binary, either in terms of experience, or in terms of group self-interest—the most obvious example of which is, again, Asian-American 'overrepresentation' in education at the elite level.

I should probably add a caveat at this point. Like the terms 'Hispanic,' 'Latino'—or 'Latinx'—to describe people in the United States who have either been born in Latin America or the Spanish-speaking countries of the Caribbean, the term 'Asian American,' or the more recent coinage 'AAPI', (that is, Asian American and Pacific Islander), only makes any kind of sense within the borders of United States. Use either term in China, and no one who does not know the USA will understand what you are talking about. That does not make them useless, but it does conceal and oversimplify a great deal. One could actually approach this from a 'semi-Woke' point of view in the sense that the demographic over-representation of Asians in elite high schools and in medical schools does not encompass all Asian American groups, while Pacific Islanders are barely represented at all outside the State of Hawaii (Pacific Islanders comprise 0.4% of the student body at Lowell High, and this is anything but an isolated example in California).

But, assuming one takes manifestos of the type McLean and DeLong have written at face value and accepts that they proffered with only the best of intentions, using the white/non-white binary is not only misleading—it is rapidly becoming (if it has not become already) a prophylactic against thought. Even their gender arguments leave a good deal to desire: DeLong and McLean do not even consider the possibility that white women might be as guilty of racism as they say white men are. To say this is emphatically not to say that white women have not suffered from misogynist bias. Of course they have. But it is to say that the role of victim and victimizer is not always stable, and that a victim can also be an authentic victimizer without making that person any less of an authentic victim. There is a wonderful *New Yorker* cartoon which shows a small fish being eaten by a medium-size fish, which in turn is being eaten by a big fish. The small fish says: "there is no justice in the world"; the medium-size fish says: "there is some justice in the world"; and the big fish says: "the world is just." It is tragic that the analytic acuity of an old cartoon is exponentially greater than that of two distinguished professors of clinical medicine.

Has systemic racial discrimination and widespread racial violence against Asian American been endemic during much of US history? Absolutely. Does such violence persist? Unquestionably—even though, in contrast to the past where this racist violence was exclusively committed by white people, often acting in the name of, or at least with the assent of, the State, today anti-Asian violence is often committed by non-whites as well (no matter what the latest proclamation from the world of ethnic studies may pretend). But what is not true, is that the crisis of inclusion can be described as one of whites versus people of color. My own view, and here I find myself yet again in improbable agreement with at least some supporters of Woke and of Critical Race Theory, is that the intractable problem the United States confronts today is Anti-Blackness. Where the solution is lies way above my pay grade. But what I am certain of is that, as long as the white/non-white binary remains the dominant way of understanding both the past and present of the USA, no solution to black exclusion will be truly effective. This should not be so hard to swallow, even for the Woke (though some of the Asian American ethnic studies people might find their livelihoods and reputations imperilled as a result). After all, the reparations movement—which I have long fervently supported—is specifically directed at African-Americans and no one else, including immigrants from Africa. And rightly so.

SENATOR ELIZABETH WARREN of Massachusetts has just sponsored a bill (S 162) called the "Anti-Racism in Public Health Act of 2021." The bill is a distillation of the ideas of people like Ibram X. Kendi, which should come as no surprise given that the public health field is where they have found a particularly receptive audience. Two elements are particularly striking. The first is its conflation of economic and psychological harms—yet another expression of the triumph of the therapeutic culture my father identified a half century ago that has morphed into what I've called 'the triumph of the traumatic.'[1] But much more repulsive is the claim that anti-racism is a science.

This is not hyperbole on my part. In the section of the bill calling for the establishment of a new structure within the Centers for Disease Control and Prevention (CDC), the National Center on Antiracism and Health, there is reference to 'the science' of anti-racism—a claim I do not believe even Kendi has ever made. The relevant passage of the bill states that one of the aims of the Center will be to,

> develop new knowledge in the science and practice of antiracism, including by identifying the mechanisms by which racism operates in the provision of health care and in systems that impact health and well-being.[2]

In other words, an ideology of White Supremacy that claimed to be based not on morality but on scientific fact is to be replaced, in US law, by an anti-racism that claims to be based not on morality but on scientific fact! Good intentions or not, the intellectual disgrace could not be more complete.

THE STUDENT UNION OF London's Westminster University has just banned whites from attending some, or all (they do not specify this in their announcement of the policy), of its Black History month events. Apparently, black students will not feel safe otherwise. In and of itself, this is an astonishing and, in my view, false instauration of black fragility.[1]

But the decision would be impossible were it not undergirded by two premises. The first is that one can't be a racist if one doesn't have power. In other words, that there is no such thing as racism of individuals but, instead, only racism of institutions and systems, though of course expressed by individuals—something one might have thought these students' daily lives would disprove to them on a daily basis. But the second is somewhat more interesting: it is the notion that the emancipatory project of our time should be, in the words of the Cambridge professor Priyamvada Gopal, to, "Abolish whiteness," and to show that "white lives don't matter as white lives." To be fair to Professor Gopal, she put her masochism where her mouth was when she also tweeted that, "I am a Brahmin. Abolish Brahmins and the upper castes. Brahmins are the whites of India," and, in another tweet, wrote that, as with whites, "Brahmin lives don't matter as Brahmin lives."[2]

Although, presumably, Professor Gopal would consider herself bitterly anti-BJP and anti-Modi, such radical binaries sound like nothing so much as Hindutva turned on its head. Doubtless, she would say that she is not for the abolition of people, but only of the institution of Brahminess, the institution of whiteness—hence her key qualifier of "*as* white" or "*as* Brahmin lives." But, in fact, this is a false self-ascription of innocence. Once you say people's lives don't matter as they themselves understand their lives—most whites, most Brahmins, etc.—but, rather, only as *you* understand them, no matter what your emancipatory intentions are, you are well on your way toward a justification of murder—just as the BJP is headed toward such a justification of murder (if it hasn't already reached it).

What is, ultimately, most striking about all this is not what I have tried to outline above but, rather, how identarian leftism and emancipatory 'anti-racism'—which see the political in everything—are not, in fact, creating a new politics but a new anti-politics.

THE JOURNAL *COMPOSITION STUDIES* identifies itself as,

> an academic journal dedicated to the range of professional practices associated with rhetoric and composition: teaching college writing; theorizing rhetoric and composing; administering writing related programs; preparing the field's future teacher-scholars.[1]

Recently, it issued a "Guide for Anti-Racist Scholarly Reviewing Practices at Composition Studies," designed to guide the *Composition Studies* editors, editorial team, reviewers, and authors toward inclusive, anti-racist editing and publishing practices. For the most part, the guidelines were predictable, up to and including the injunction that, "[b]ibliographies that only cite white scholars are unacceptable." The journal also trumpets that it no longer will require the use of what it refers to as 'canonical citations,' on the grounds that,

> [w]e understand the authors of some such texts may have engaged in harmful and/or oppressive actions.[2]

For 'canonical' read authoritative. What is meant here, is that the biography of a scholar trumps the quality of the scholarship or, more precisely, that the two are inseparable. That this is what constitutes 'anti-racism' is a testimony not to the closing of the American mind—for what an optimist Allan Bloom has turned out to be—but, rather, to its assisted suicide. But the journal has a problem. It is committed to the rooting out of racism, especially from the peer review process, and boasts of its reliance on what it terms MMUs: a relatively new 'anti-racist' acronym that stands for the Multiply Marginalized and Underrepresented. The journal's problem is that, while on the one hand it declares itself to be,

> committed to listening to and believing MMU reviewers and their perspectives, especially regarding a piece they feel is bigoted, exclusionary, or does not engage deeply with relevant scholarship by MMU scholars,

it worries that MMU reviewers may come into "contact with potentially bigoted or traumatic material." Therefore, it pledges to provide prospective [MMU] reviewers "with the abstract of the piece we are asking them to review," thus offering them "the opportunity to decline reading it."

Adorno writes somewhere that, "[i]ntolerance of ambiguity is the mark of an authoritarian personality." That intolerance is in full display in the journal's guidelines. Equally evident is the extent to which the concept of trauma has become one of the central organizing principles of the emancipatory movements of the age.

THERE IS AN EXCELLENT PIECE by Amna Khalid and Jeffrey Aaron Snyder in the usually dependably Woke *Chronicle of Higher Education*,[1] which cuts through the all-too-common wishful thinking: that, somehow, with enough good will, a strong form of academic freedom and a strong form of 'inclusion'—as understood by the DEI lens that prevails today on virtually all US university campuses—can be reconciled. Their concluding paragraph definitively refutes these consoling fictions:

> When institutions proclaim that academic freedom and inclusion coexist in a kind of synergistic harmony, they are trafficking in PR-driven wishful thinking.

In the hardest cases, there is no way of upholding an 'all are welcome here' brand of inclusion, while simultaneously defending academic freedom. Instead, we should turn to the wise words of Hanna Holborn Gray, former president of the University of Chicago:

> Education should not be intended to make people comfortable, it is meant to make them think.

The problem with Khalid and Snyder's analysis, as well as with their prescriptions, is not that these are wrong. To the contrary, it seems to me that were they to be accepted, something that would involve a radical reduction in the power of DEI bureaucracies and a radical transformation of students' expectations that they have the right not to be offended, universities would actually be able to do their job properly—as is most emphatically not the case today. But the task is a far more difficult one than even Khalid and Snyder allow. They posit the conflict as being one taking place within universities—which is true—but seem to suggest that it can be rectified within universities—which, I'm afraid, is false. This is because, although the model for what Khalids and Snyder call 'DEI Inc.' is indeed largely speaking the reification within the academe not just of a particular set of emancipatory ideas and expectations as defined by the identitarian left and demotic Critical Race Theory. Those ideas and expectations reflect those of the culture as a whole, and long predate the ideological takeover of universities that Khalid and Snyder are rightly appalled by.

They know this, of course. And in this their view is thankfully oceans apart from the conspiracy-theorizing of too many critics of the DEI catastrophe, whose cultural and intellectual consequences within the academe have indeed justified the worst fears of conservative intellectuals like Allan Bloom and my father (I was unforgivably slow in recognizing this). But, where Bloom, Philip Rieff, and many contemporary conservative critics went wrong was in seeing the university as something that could exist at an intellectual and cultural remove from the culture at large. Such views, to put it bluntly, are impermissibly romantic, both about the autonomy of the life of the mind, and about the sacerdotal role that should be the professoriate's right. Universities have *always* reflected the dominant culture, and have changed—albeit usually with some lag time—as it has changed. The rigidly hierarchical university of Wilhelmine Germany gave way not because it lost its nerve (conservatives always fetishize the role of the will; it is one of the most incorrigibly sentimental aspects of their worldview), but because the rigidly hierarchical society that had given rise to it collapsed. If the liberal university of today is collapsing—and it is—this is not because it has been undermined from within by cells of scheming Marcuseans in a long march through the institutions, Critical Race theorists, etc. It is all much more straightforward: the liberal university has collapsed because liberalism as the governing consensus of US and Canadian society has collapsed.

It is not that Khalid and Snyder fail to understand this. As they put it in their essay:

> Education is a product: students are consumers, and campus diversity is a customer-service issue that needs to be administered from the top down. ("Chief diversity officers," according to an article in *Diversity Officer Magazine*, "are best defined as 'change-management specialists.'") DEI Inc. purveys a safety-and-security model of learning that is highly attuned to harm and that conflates respect for minority students with unwavering affirmation and validation.[2]

And, yet, tough-minded as they are, Khalid and Snyder still think that the university can resist the transformation of the culture at large, and that the professoriate can regain what they call "the *right* to decide what and how to teach based on their academic expertise and their pedagogical goals," and that students, DEI administrators and other campus stakeholders can be made to understand this. Of course, I hope they are right—but I can't see how they possibly can be. Ours is a culture in which the battle between feeling and reason, and between objectivity and subjectivity, have been lost; in which health and safety are fetishized (even though in reality we have less and less of either); in which adults don't want to grow up and, in parallel, in which the feelings of children about themselves—above all, but not only about their gender identities—are thought to be dispositive; in which, just as Guy Debord predicted, the whole of social life has been commodified, including feelings, including dissent.

This is what is sounding the last post for academic freedom and, more broadly, for the intellect and for the high culture to which the academe once offered a home. Vile though it is, and destructive as it is within the academe, DEI is a manifestation of the collapse, not its cause. And all this is before the full post-human weight of AI begins to make itself felt.

THE ACADEMIC SENATE for California Community Colleges (ASCCC)[1] is the official professional organization representing faculty throughout the state's community college system. It was instrumental in drafting the official California community College "Model Principles and Practices for Diversity, Equity and Inclusion in Curriculum." The document itself is a kind of *summum bonum* of the conventional wisdom of the age in education—one in which education in the conventional sense of imparting skills, knowledge, etc. isn't even mentioned in the ASCCC's 'vision statement' which, instead, declares itself to be one of "Faculty leading change, serving students, and advancing equity, anti-racism, and accessibility."

This is not surprising, given that the 'Model Principles' document is partly dedicated to contrasting what it calls "Traditional Educational Practice," with its "harmful legacy" of institutional racism and Eurocentrism, with "Culturally Responsive Classroom Practices." One of the former, it appears, is academic freedom as conventionally understood. The authors of the document are quite explicit on this point. "Take care," they warn,

> not to 'weaponize' academic freedom and academic integrity as tools to impede equity in an academic discipline or influct curricular trauma on our students, especially historically marginalized students.[2]

Of course, what is actually being weaponized in our culture as an increasingly successful method for suppressing any real diversity of view is not academic freedom, but trauma.

TO DISAGREE IS TO TRAUMATIZE. The Triumph of the Traumatic is also the banalization of the traumatic. A case in point is the University of California San Francisco (UCSF) "Task Force Report on Equity and Anti-Racism in Research." The report itself will not surprise anyone familiar with the ideology of the DEI bureaucracy, or the particular version of this worldview that now dominates the US medical establishment in medical universities and research centers like UCSF. As the report puts it in its opening:

> What has been supported and valued, how research has been executed, as well as who leads and engages in research has limited health outcomes for far too many people. We came together to address these harms at UCSF, to find a path forward to center the research needs and engagement of those marginalized at all levels of the research enterprise.[1]

What is striking is that the report begins by highlighting in the Foreword the way those preparing it had been traumatized by the work itself and by negative reactions that were received from colleagues commenting on the draft. "It is extremely important to acknowledge," wrote the Task Force's co-chair, the public health specialist and deputy director of UCSF's Global Health Institute, Sun Yu Cotter,

> the magnitude of the emotional labor and trauma that many of the Task Force members endured in doing this work, particularly during the public comment period." Task Force members, Cotter lamented, "especially our Black colleagues, [encounter and navigate racism on a

daily basis at work and outside of work." And, she added, "we are also volunteering our very limited time to dive into gruelling work (the minority tax is real!).[2]

This was bad enough. But then "to be gaslit by some members of our very own UCSF community was very painful." However, Cotter added,

> Drs. McLemore and Nguyen [the Task Force's other co-chairs] held space for us as a Task Force to be present, sit with the pain and hurt, wipe our tears, take a deep collective breath, embrace one another, and keep going because we know we can't give up.[3]

The conviction that to volunteer to shape a project that states as its goal the devising of an actual plan that, as Dr. Nguyen put it,

> can guide the research enterprise at UCSF to have an inclusive, diverse, and equitable environment with the goal of advancing health for all diverse communities,[4]

is a sacrifice that task force members deserve credit for agreeing to make, and, indeed, should have been remunerated financially for making, is quite astonishing. On the one hand, the report is existentially important: a roadmap for what, in the DEI lexicon, is called the time of 'racial reckoning' in the United States. On the other hand, however, doing the work is traumatizing in and of itself, and having colleagues "[deny] the existence of inequities and racism, and others that minimize the burden that racism has imposed," is more traumatizing still.

One tries in vain to think of any other social movement with as radical a transformative agenda as DEI that has ever so deeply and, above all, so ostentatiously, felt so sorry for itself. It is not just that the personal and the political have become inextricably entangled; it is that the most self-indulgent, therapeutized conception of the personal and the most utopian conception of the political have become inextricably entangled. In a century, the American left apparently has moved from 'Don't Mourn, Organize,' 'to 'I'm Organizing, so don't traumatize me or I may not be able to do so successfully.'

One tries to imagine Lenin seeking praise for having overcome the pain and hurt that he felt in order to go to the Finland Station, or even having needed to stop for a session of his encounter group in order to find the courage to make his way there. But that is just what the members of the UCSF apparently do expect. This is not a revolution, it's a tantrum.

A SOCIETY IN MORAL FREE FALL will eventually go into intellectual free fall as well. This point has been reached in the Anglosphere, sooner or later to be followed by the other post-Protestant countries of Northern Europe. The irony is that the architects of this intellectual free fall sincerely believe themselves to be justice-seekers, not vandals. If anything, this is now even more true in the STEM fields than in the humanities, although this may simply be because no one really understands anymore what the humanities are good for—and, as a result, they are dying—whereas everyone understands that in the twenty-first century STEM subjects are indispensable. As Jerry Coyne and Luana Maroja have put it:

> Scientists both inside and outside the academy were among the first to begin politically purging their fields by misrepresenting or even lying about inconvenient truths. Campaigns were launched to strip scientific jargon of words deemed offensive, to ensure that results that could 'harm' people seen as oppressed were removed from research manuscripts, and to tilt the funding of science away from research and toward social reform. The American government even refused to make genetic data—collected with taxpayer dollars—publicly available if analysis of that data could be considered 'stigmatizing.'[1]

But laying the lion's share of blame at Woke's doorstep does Woke too much honor. The ethically motived purges that Coyne and Maroja—mistakenly—take to be political are, in fact, the 'sealing of the deal' of the triumph of a therapeutic culture that of course long predates Woke. Because they originate in academic culture, these contemporary manifestations are particularly two-dimensional and fevered, and bear Weber's contention in "Science as a Vocation" that, "Academic prophecy will create only fanatical sects but never a genuine community."[2] But, even without Woke, the post-Protestant world would still never have been capable of resisting the therapeutic tide. Its triumph would have taken a bit longer, that's all.

Coyne and Maroja rightly refer to the new reluctance within the STEM world to study subjects or, even if studies have been done, to release their data and findings that might stigmatize or otherwise be harmful to oppressed and 'marginalized' groups within society. But, in a culture obsessed with recognition, stigmatization is intolerable. To the contrary, everyone must be celebrated by society as a whole. As the California Attorney General, Rob Bonta, put it in his official statement celebrating Pride Month:

> As a committed LGBTQ+ ally, I firmly believe that everyone deserves to be safe, healthy, prosperous, and celebrated for who they are—regardless of how they identify or who they love.[3]

That no one is startled by the idea that everyone should be publicly celebrated for who they are is actually quite extraordinary. Of course, people should be privately celebrated as such by loved ones and co-workers. But, to say everyone must be celebrated for who they are, is to say that, as a polity, celebration is a kind of moral and social debt owed to every individual and every group. But, again, in post-Protestant culture such expectations long predate Woke, the postulate of intersectionality, and Critical Race Theory. Think of one of the most popular American pop songs of the 1970s, Ray Stevens's "Everything is Beautiful in its Own Way."[4]

Of course, to say that everything is beautiful, or that everyone needs to be celebrated for who they are, is to make the concept of beauty (or, indeed, of celebration) utterly meaningless. Similarly, if everyone needs to be celebrated all the time, what does celebration even mean? And, yet, *not* being told one is beautiful or that one should be celebrated is unbearable in a therapeutized culture such as this one. It upsets people's sense of well-being, and that well-being, as my father wrote in 1987 in his *The Triumph of the Therapeutic*, the

> sense of well-being has become the end, rather that a by-product of striving after some superior communal end.[5]

Thus have being human and being celebrated for the way in which one is human become inextricably linked. And, by the same token, not being celebrated, thought beautiful, etc. becomes an unbearable affront, which does much to explain why we live in a society where so many people constantly feel affronted, offended, or on the verge of being so. Only Niagaras of praise are morally acceptable.

And it is a short step between wanting to be celebrated and wanting to be a celebrity. In that sense, Andy Warhol's prediction that everyone would be famous for fifteen minutes is a better place to start if one wants to understand the cultural disaster that has taken place than Ibram Kendi or Robin DiAngelo's Woke nostrums.

HAVING BEEN TRAUMATIZED is moving from an explanatory key to something the young are expected to feel (and express), whether in reality they do or they don't—particularly when applying for admission to university. Confirmation of this is easy to find. On the website of the IACAC (the Illinois Association for College Admission Counseling), one finds an entry called "Addressing Trauma in the College Essay," which turns out to be an account of a workshop on the subject that the author (a guidance counselor, as they used to be called in less euphemism-drenched times), named Cody Dailey, from Victor J. Andrew High School in suburban Chicago, attended that had been organized by the National Association for College Admission Counseling. Boilerplate pieties aside, what is striking is that the expectation that a student will write about their trauma is now so well-established, such a cultural norm, that the author feels duty-bound to remind his colleagues that students must not be made to feel that it's absolutely obligatory for them to do so.

"Among the key takeaways," Cody Dailey writes,

> there was a reminder that students should not feel required or pressured into always writing about their challenges. While that is a powerful topic to explore, there are many others, including writing about a passion, an identity, a career, an important object or memory, or even a unique skill or 'superpower.' Sometimes students feel pigeon-holed into writing about their traumas, but we should remind them that they own the distribution rights to those moments."[1]

The superpower of suffering?

THERAPEUTIC LANGUAGE HAS long been the *lingua franca* of US society (and increasingly that of the entire Anglosphere). And traumatic language is therapeutic language further weaponized and deployed. It should, therefore, come as no surprise that the anti-Woke legislation that the governor of Florida, Ron DeSantis, is now proposing is as reliant on therapeutic language as any DEI official at a US university or facilitator at any DiAngelo-style 'anti-racism' workshop. For example, the "Stop W.O.K.E. Act" (the acronym stands for "Stop Wrongs to Our Kids and Employees Act") includes a provision banning any teaching that would lead "an individual [to] feel discomfort, guilt, anguish, or any other form of psychological distress on account of his or her race, color, sex, or national origin."[1]

Some opponents of the bill, and even some who support it, have ironized that the right is now mimicking the language of Woke, whether grotesquely (as the critics say), or as a form of payback (as some of the bill's supporters have said). This, though, represents a misunderstanding of the US crisis. For Americans of both the right and the left have almost no other language that they can turn to that still seems truthful, no appeal for justice or redress that does not seem immensely strengthened and made more authoritative, than appealing to the unfalsifiable fevers of the subjective. That this is a catastrophe for thought and, by extension, for our politics, should be obvious.

WE NOW LIVE IN A CULTURE in which not to consider yourself a victim is a pathology—perhaps the only remaining one, everything else being simply a different and as such inherently laudable state of consciousness—or else, whether you realize it or not, or are willing to admit to it or not, it is to be an oppressor.

THE TRIUMPH OF THE TRAUMATIC—which expands the idea of trauma to the point of its being seen as the source of almost every form of human unhappiness—is, also, the Triumph of the Metaphoric, in the sense that it largely rejects any suggestion that there is a morally significant distinction to be drawn between the physical and the verbal. Metaphoriztion is the order of the day across the academic-cultural-philanthropic complex. But, nowhere has it become more central than in the rhetoric of traumatic culture's identitarian avant-garde, the trans movement, in which it is now taken as self-evident that any verbal rejection of the trans movement's claims about gender by the so-called Gender Critical Movement of anti-trans Feminists is, in and of itself, indistinguishable in any important moral sense from acts of physical violence against trans people. A representative expression of it can be found in the Lemkin Institute for Genocide Prevention's 2022 "Statement on the Genocidal Nature of the Gender Movement's Ideology and Practice":

> While members of the Gender Critical Movement may argue that they do not seek to kill the physical bodies of transgender people, they do openly seek to eradicate transgender identity in the world.[1]

The statement's use of the term 'physical bodies,' rather than just 'bodies'—presumably to distinguish them from 'spiritual bodies'—is itself emblematic of the new hegemony of the metaphorical, down which the Lemkin Institute statement toboggans at Mach 2. To contest trans identity is held to deny it, and to deny it is held to be no different than wanting to eradicate it. As such, it is genocidal. Of course, this argument depends on making those who define themselves as trans members of a people every bit as much as this can be said of European Jews or of Rwandan Tutsis—and considering the attempts by Nazis and Hutu to exterminate them to be ideologically no different than those of Gender Critical Feminism denials of trans identity, which the statement actually singles out as "*particularly* genocidal" [italics mine], though 'particularly' as compared to what is not specified.

The Lemkin Institute statement does concede that, so far at least, there has been no attempt at the mass slaughter of trans people—however, it warns that this might very well follow were Gender Critical Movement to prevail. But it likens the denial of trans identity to the residential boarding schools in the US, Canada, and Australia that sought to destroy the cultural identities of the indigenous children who were forced to reside in them. But, even this comparison depends on believing that 'soul murder' is not fundamentally different than physical murder. As such, it is the ultimate triumph of the metaphorical understanding of the world in the strict sense that the great literary theorist I. A. Richards meant when he described metaphor as being the "carrying over of a word from its normal use to a new use," and as a "transaction between contexts."[2]

The problem is that, while such transactions may pose no danger in a work of literature, to carry over from its normal use to a new use the word 'genocide' or, indeed, of any term meant only to describe physical suffering and death in reality is a transaction between contexts that is being transacted with the counterfeit coin of bad faith.

UTOPIA AND REVOLUTION are often confused. When I say that I am an anti-utopian, readers of my work who may otherwise agree with me in important ways still demand to know how I can make such a claim when history clearly demonstrates that transformations of both the social order and of the moral consensus that for centuries have seemed inconceivable at least sometimes come to pass. And, about history leaving room for the most improbable transformations, they are right: slavery was generally considered to be an immutable part of the order for almost all of human history until, within the space of only less than three hundred years, it came to be seen as wholly illegitimate. The same can be said about the subjugation of women by men. So, if what utopia means is simply the ever-present possibility of change, then no one—at least no one who does not think all positive changes have already been made—should call themselves an anti-utopian.

But there is a second definition of utopia that propounds a secular version of the religious idea of redemption, and imagines a society from which all human cares have disappeared. That is the form of utopianism that I have spent most of my long life as a writer trying to call into question.

Feminism is a powerful iteration of the first type of utopianism. When Feminists in the 1970s insisted that the personal was the political, they were making an argument about power and justice. Their position was that any society that did not transform the power relations of the private life—male dominance and female subordination—could not at the most fundamental level be considered just, no matter what other transformations it succeeded in achieving. But, saying the personal was the political has since been taken to mean that *everything* is political. And this is the utopianism of the object—that is, the objective correlative is society.

What we seem to have entered of late, though, is something very different: a utopianism of the subject. It is not simply that all identities are in flux, for this is often the case in moments of social upheaval. Rather, it is that each individual has absolute control over their own identity—a control entirely based on how they feel. An emblematic case is the widespread re-evaluation of the nature of sex and gender that the trans movement has put forward, and now commands a great deal of influence not just in the academic world, but in medicine—above all in obstetrics and gynaecology—and in public health.

It is now taken as a given in the mainstream medical world that sex and gender are distinct categories. In the Children's Health section of the (*very* mainstream) Mayo Clinic website, for example, it is simply taken as a matter of scientific fact that,

> [a] particular sex assigned at birth or gender expression doesn't mean a person has any specific gender identity or sexual orientation.[1]

More militant physicians go much further. For example, discussing ultrasound, Justin Brandt, a physician at Rutgers University specializing in maternal-fetal medicine, told an interviewer from the MedPage website that, "[u]ltrasound presents an opportunity to promote use of accurate language around fetal sex versus fetal gender." What he proposed was saying the following to a patient:

> [W]e can identify whether there are genitalia that appear male or female, but we cannot identify this baby's gender. This child will tell us his or her or their gender, when this child is ready to describe how they feel.[2]

Even leaving aside Dr. Brandt's stacking of the rhetorical deck by using the word 'appear' (as if, somehow, even this identification was suspect), what is striking here is the belief that there is no significant distinction to be drawn between what one feels and what one is. This is not just the triumph of the therapeutic; it is the dictatorship of the therapeutic—as if, what we feel, once we discover it, from then on becomes immutable. Does this mean there is no such thing as body dysphoria? Obviously it doesn't—but the numbers are actually quite small. Many transgender activists agree with this. For example, in a recent opinion piece in the *New York Daily News*, the transgender activist Sean Ebony Coleman called on New York City's new mayor, Eric Adams, to "appoint [a] transgender person to a key leadership position [in his administration]."[3] This, Coleman argued, was necessary for transgender New Yorkers to be fairly represented. But the figure Coleman gave for the number of transgender people in all of New York State was "90,000," in other words 0.45% of the state's nearly twenty million residents.

But this has not prevented the sacralization of the subjective to steadily proceed. In a way, all this is very American, in the sense that it has always been part of American's imagined contract with the Zeitgeist that one can be who one wants to be. What changes with the trans movement is its embrace of a subjective essentialism—however contradictory the melding of those two ideas may appear at first glance. The idea is not so much that one chooses whom one wants to be—that there are "no second acts in American lives," as F. Scott Fitzgerald famously put it—but, rather, that it is by understanding the real nature of one's own feelings about oneself that one will be able to identify whom one is.

And the idea that one could be mistaken about any of this is rejected out of hand. This is why trans activists—or, rather, 'proponents of gender-affirming surgery', to use the preferred terminology of the movement—are so sincerely untroubled by the idea of very young people putting themselves on severe chemical regimens to prevent, or halt, the onset of puberty, and to be able to opt for very radical surgical procedures that can never be undone. And, if they really believe that a self-identification of something as fundamental of one's gender once arrived at is beyond question, then there is indeed no moral issue.

But is this the case? Or was Leonard Cohen closer to the essence of the human condition when in one of his songs he declaimed, "I distrust my inner feelings/Inner feelings come and go"? Judith Thurman has put the matter with great clarity, writing that,

> [u]topian thinking becomes tyrannical, as opposed to merely wishful, when it denies the paradoxes of human nature. And human nature is founded on paradox. Indeed, it is founded on the paradoxes we experience in our dream life. That surely is one of the great problems

> with Wokeness. it denies the truths we repress or forget when we 'wake.'[4]

But for some by then it will be too late.

IN A WORLD WHERE THERE IS little job security, and where being an entrepreneur, rather than climbing the proverbial corporate ladder, is regarded as the surest way to succeed in life, it should come as no surprise that people increasingly have the same entrepreneurial attitude toward their identities—above all, of course, to their gender identities. Early Freudians like Sándor Ferenczi posited that, in order to get to a point of accepting reality, small children had to abandon their previous stage that was characterized by feelings of omnipotence.[1] Without this transition, Ferenczi thought that children would never be able to become adults. The image he used for this refusal was the Scottish playwright J. M. Barrie's character Peter Pan, "the boy who would never grow" and, instead, wants only to live in his idyllic 'Neverland.' Ferenczi thought it something that largely affected profoundly traumatized children, a term he did not use in the expansive sense in which it is used today. For him, because they would never be able to live adult lives, such children were tragic figures, doomed to failure as adults, by which Ferenczi meant failure in life.

But today, it often seems as if it is those who aspire to omnipotence, rather than those who bend to reality, who are most amply rewarded. Before his fall, Sam Bankman-Fried seemed to exemplify this change: the boy genius who makes billions of dollars while being quite literally dressed like a child and often speaking like a child in one of Ferenczi's case books. Bankman-Fried turned out to be running a Ponzi scheme, but 'Bankman-Friedism'—the idea that you didn't have to grow up to be hugely successful—is very much alive and well. All of this was prefigured in Penny Marshall's 1983 film *Big*, in which the main character, Josh Baskin, is a twelve-year-old who makes a wish that he will turn into an adult and is indeed transformed into one. The denouement is consolingly conventional: Josh finds out he doesn't want to be 'big' and is transformed into a child again and reunited with his parents. But, in the interim, Josh becomes an executive at a toy company which he provides with brilliant idea after brilliant idea.

Penny Marshall and her scriptwriters, Garry Ross and Anne Spielberg, stacked the deck by making the firm a toy company. But the tech world remains a world full of Josh Baskins. At the very least, the era is long gone where the dominant was that work and pleasure need to be kept separate or, more precisely, as Adorno described it, both proper work and proper pleasure required that,

> no instinctual aberrations will interfere with seriousness of rational behavior, no signs of seriousness and responsibility will cast their shadow over the fun.[2]

And, in an echo of Ferenczi, Adorno noted that,

> the libidinization of gadgets is indirectly narcissistic in as much as it feeds on the ego's control of nature: gadgets provide the subject with some memories of early feelings of omnipotence.[3]

But, today, far from being irrational denials of reality, the successful entrepreneur is unlikely to succeed without a childish—which is to say, an irrational—sense of the possible. And, in our culture, this will to impose oneself, to 'disrupt,'—to use the business school term of art as implacably as a small child having a tantrum—brings not a spanking but material reward. At the same time, the destruction of the distinction between the personal and the political, which begins with 1970s Feminism, but has long since been well and truly commodified, has led to the collapse of the belief that reality must always trump fantasy.

That is why subjective idealism—the conviction that only minds and mental contents really matter—has become the default philosophical position of our age. Yes, a human being experiences material things, but these are nothing more than perceptions; in short, if one thinks it, it is so; or, at least, can be made to become so. The trans movement's insistence that—in the words of a trans blogger who used to go by the hard to forget name Lithium Labia (now Fae The Evil Bisexual)—"like some women don't have dicks, and some men don't have vaginas!"[4] makes no sense until you put it in the context of subjective idealism, at which point it makes all too much sense. Just as the entrepreneur's role is the disruption—the 'creative destruction' of all business certainties—so the trans movement is engaged in the disruption and creative disruption of the certainties of sex and gender.

This culture may appear balkanized and incoherent, and in some ways it is. But in other ways it is remarkably unified and, really, quite coherent.

A CANADIAN SOCIAL WORKER named Kaeden Seburn has written and posted on his website[1] a document titled "Introduction to Gender Identity and Expression: A Webinar for Parents and Caregivers." Seburn's self-description is of being "a nonbinary, transmasculine, white settler, and a trans community organizer, activist and educator from unceded Algonquin territory." In the Ontario universities that he attended (Bachelor in Social Work from Carleton, Master's from York), such self-portraits are fairly standard these days. So is the explicit insistence that children, and not just adolescents, should be the sole arbiters. "If a child or youth tells you that they are trans or non-binary," Seburn declares flatly, "then they are. Children of any age can know or determine their gender identity."[2]

For Seburn, this means that children should not only be able to identify as they see fit, but also that no one should have the right to challenge such self-identification. "Trans children and youth are the experts in their own lives,"[3] Seburn insists, and they alone make the decisions about the way they express this identity. This includes having access to "transition related services such as hormones and surgery when they request it." And Seburn notes that in Ontario there is no minimum age of consent for health care decisions and therefore "youth"—from the context, it is apparent he is very much including children—"can make decisions about their own care and their own bodies,"[4] without any need for any detailed medical assessment. Next to these sentences, there is a Manga-style cartoon of a youth saying, "A trans kid's gender expression shouldn't be doctors choice."[5]

The moral and cultural arguments Seburn makes are fairly standard fare these days. What is more profound in historical terms is that the contemporary redefinition of sex and gender is also a redefinition of childhood. One must be very careful here. As the great French historian Philippe Ariès showed in his book *Centuries of Childhood*,[6] childhood is conventionally understood today as a separate and distinct phase of life in which one's offspring are entitled to special care and attention within the family circle. Before that, Ariès argued, by the age of seven children were largely treated as miniature adults.[7]

One of the lasting legacies of the transformation of the conception of sex and gender—assuming that it endures (as I believe it will)—will be at least a partial return to something not all that different before what Ariès called "the invention of childhood." This is not to say that what is happening came like the proverbial bolt out of the blue. The advent, by the 1980s at the latest, of what the French call *'l'enfant roi'*—where instead of controlling their children, parents increasingly have let their children control them—already marked a profound transformation in the understanding of the nature of childhood (and, of course, of adulthood as well). In this sense, the leap is not that great between the acceptance of the idea that children should be able to decide most things for themselves to the idea that children should be able to define themselves as they, and they alone, see fit—even, when necessary, through hormones and surgery.

Viewed in isolation, saying that children should have the right to take drugs to prevent puberty or have what is euphemistically called 'gender affirming' surgery may seem like a social earthquake. But, just as there is an increasing scientific consensus that big earthquakes only occur after there have been a series of smaller ones, so the current redefinition of childhood—one that would make more sense to people in Europe before the seventeenth century than would the reigning idea about the nature of childhood in, say, 1950—was unquestionably preceded by its own less powerful disturbances. And, in any case, if adults no longer accept the burdens of responsibility that come with being an adult, why should children accept the traditional limitations that come with being a child?

FOR ALL ITS TALK OF intersectionality, the identitarian view of the world is in reality one in which every member of every group speaks for their own demographic alone. And, since no one who is not a member of the identity group in question can be expected to understand that group's experience, it becomes the moral and intellectual equivalent of patent law in the sense that, to use as an example what has become an article of faith in the Woke cultural establishment—above all in literature—for a white person to write about black people is a form of moral copyright infringement. This finds its echo in the Woke takeover of psychoanalysis, in which it is assumed that one's psychic difficulties largely derive from the way, or ways, in which one has been oppressed (or, failing that, the psychic burden of one's privilege). There are no individuals, just members of oppressed or oppressing collectivities.

In such a framing, self-understanding is largely historical and sociological. A century ago, when he assumed the rectorship of the UNAM (Mexico's national university), José Vasconcelos wrote, "For my race, my spirit will speak"—a dictum that became the UNAM's motto. The racial, gender, sexual, and ethnic identitarians of today are largely ignorant of Vasconcelos, but they are his inheritors. And the art they produce (though agit-prop is not just a better characterization, it is the only accurate one) reflects this notion that individual expression, like the individual psyche, is an artifact of oppression that needs to be understood as such, and demolished for being so. As a result, we have art that is not just wholly didactic, with no room for transcendence (as even the most didactic religious art has almost always been), but innocent of ambivalence. In other words, Kitsch.

THE TRANS MOVEMENT'S RUPTURE with the past could not be more radical in its insistence that, with some exceptions—whose number trans activists are given to wildly exaggerating—while a person's biological sex can be established with authority by someone other than oneself, one's gender is whatever one feels it to be. But trans' radicalism overshadows what should be obvious, which is that, in an important sense, trans ideology is less of a break with the past than is generally assumed—above all in the ways that it recapitulates the Wellness movement, though in a politicized and defiantly antinomian way. For, the key doctrine in Wellness is that of what its followers call 'self-care,' and which the historian Natalia Petrzela (who teaches modern US history at the New School for Social Research in New York and is a proselytizer for the benefits of the Wellness perspective) has described as,

> the idea that our own minds, bodies, and nature (rather than experts and chemical treatments) hold the keys to optimizing health and happiness.[1]

To put it another way, the fundamental premise of Wellness is that it is not a a doctor—or, for that matter, society at large—but rather *you*, the individual, and only you, who knows how you feel and what's best for you: subjective well-being is well-being.

Unlike Trans, the Wellness Movement is now totally mainstream (though it is anything but out of the question that trans eventually gets to that point as well). Wellness is now a multi-billion dollar industry.[2] It is also one of America's most triumphantly successful exports, and demonstrates (as the internationalization of Woke does as well) that American cultural hegemony, even in this age of negative exceptionalism, is still largely intact, at least across the Anglosphere. And yet at the time of its inception in the nineteen-seventies Wellness, too, was very much a fringe movement.

Trans has another source as well, which is the American idea that you can reinvent yourself more or less at will. In 1941, F. Scott Fitzgerald wrote in his unfinished novel, *The Last Tycoon*, that, "There are no second acts in American lives." It is an assumption that today's trans movement incarnates. Trans' synthesis of Wellness and the American conviction that one can be whatever one as an individual chooses to be is one of its less noticed, but most original characteristics. And the bridge between these two ideas, what makes them so comfortably miscible today, is what my father called 'the triumph of the therapeutic.'

For, at its most fundamental, therapeutic culture is about discovering what you really feel, and by extension whom you really are. To be sure, trans in practice also involves the commodification of identity. But, I think, the movement's critics have overemphasized this aspect of trans and underemphasized the fact that it is about finding one's true self, no matter what anyone else thinks. Where the therapeutic comes in, is through the generalization, in its contemporary iteration, of the idea of trauma. For, once you come to assume that not deferring to your subjective feelings will cause you physical—as well as mental—harm, anything less than full acceptance by society of the idea that what, subjectively, you feel yourself to be should be the beginning and end of the public debate, becomes a public health crisis, and, as it is becoming in law, also a matter of people's civil rights.

The ghost at the banquet, though, is that old Marxian standby: alienation. Because the identitarian assumption, most radically and imperiously exemplified by trans, is that alienation is at its root caused in large measure by society's failure to accept all identities people claim for themselves, and, as a morally and politically necessary consequence of this, to 'represent' and, indeed, to celebrate them. The poverty of the identitarian analysis of class derives from this misunderstanding, or, if one wants to be generous, this monochromatic and self-referential understanding of alienation. The right to self-fulfillment is a category mistake. There can be no such right, if for no other reason then that there is no society on earth that is capable of providing and no prospect in this age of disasters, of the climate calamity, the resurgence of war, and the beginnings (yes, only the beginnings) of a wave of migrations that will, and sooner rather than later I would wager, transform every single one of the world's nations and their national and regional cultures, no matter how particular, vibrant, and firmly established. In contrast, alienation can only increase in these conditions, something that the identitarian band aid, if it is even that, will not even palliate.

BOUTIQUE RIGHTS FOR boutique identities. One of the cardinal assumptions of the Progressive left—and of much of that part of contemporary liberalism whose moral beacon remains the human rights movement—is that, where there is a need, there is a right. There is much to question regarding this view, above all its out of hand dismissal of any suggestion that installing a legal regime of rights in the poor world that include those rights that states simply do not have the means to provide, at least not fully—guaranteed incomes, say, or even, in the poorest countries, decent housing and adequate nutrition—is one of the ways in which the ideals of the Global North complacently ignore the realities of the Global South (as well as indulging in the human rights movement's greatest intellectual and moral solecism, which is to insist that the anti-politics of international law offers an escape hatch from the rigors and uncertainties of actual politics). But, as long as the general claim that 'where there is a need, there is a right' concerned material needs, such as the right to food or shelter—that is to say, needs that can be measured and quantified—it enjoyed a measure of coherence.

Now, however, the radical subjectivity that is at the core of identity politics has shattered all that. For, while it is possible to agree on, say, how much food a person needs to thrive, it is impossible for anyone—save for the person or the group expressing the need—to say how much recognition, or affirmation, or sense of psychic security they need, or, as they would say, are entitled to. But it should be obvious that it is impossible to correlate the contemporary expansion of needs with a similar expansion in the number of rights. And, yet—as this is exactly what many Progressives are in fact demanding—it should be equally obvious that it is not.

In a world in which every desire is to be treated as a right—as increasingly is the case in the rich world—rights will soon lose their original meaning, if they have not already; and, sooner rather than later, any meaning at all beyond a legally enforceable demand for utter credulity in the name of equity and emancipation. The old joke about the man searching for a way out after having been caught *in flagrante* by his wife says to her, "Whom are you going to believe, me or your lying eyes," has been turned on its head: now you are expected to dismiss whatever it is you see if it does not conform with what you are told you are seeing.

THE HEART'S MORONIC TYRANNY proceeds apace. Forget the ravages of the post-structuralists, the willful misinterpreters of Foucault, the performative nonsense—nihilism mistaking itself for a higher moralism—that lies at the heart of Judith Butler's work, and now dominates the academic humanities. Americans never cared much for the life of the mind, anyway. That is why there has been so little opposition to the ecstatic philistinism of identity politics that has now swept everything before it in the US, and, because, for all the talk of a post-American world, US cultural hegemony is still so total in Europe and in Latin America, not just in the post-Protestant countries of the Anglosphere, Scandinavia, and Holland, but in post-Catholic countries of those regions as well. For, when all is said and done, Woke largely consists of the old Babbitry in which the old axiom of small town White Protestant America—"If you don't have something nice to say, don't say anything at all"—has been redeployed in the service of supposed emancipation and reparation. And beneath that lies the old American incapacity of distinguishing between wish and reality, and the rage provoked by any thwarting of any American wish, no matter how garishly preposterous. Whatever I say I am, I am. Deny that and you are denying me: that's the mantra. And in our great times, woe betide anyone who falls afoul of it. Objective correlative? What objective correlative?

IT USED TO BE A PSYCHIATRIC commonplace, that both the infantile personality and the hysterical one were characterized by exhibitionism, self-dramatization, diffuse forms of eroticism, and the desire to control others by wielding an individual's suffering as a weapon. 'The 'Triumph of the Traumatic' is the rise to preeminence in contemporary bourgeois culture (in Global North, but in much of the Global South as well) of these toxic personality types. Of course, such people do not think of themselves as hysterics—et alone as tantrum-throwing infants—but, rather, as people seeking justice in an unjust world, who are also committed to building a better one. And their vehicle for this has been what is often called Woke, but is better understood as a mustering for roll call of a vast army of the wronged that believes our time is the era of reckoning.

That this is to a large extent a post-Christian spin on Christian millenarianism should be obvious: the last shall be first and the first shall be last, and so on. But, though the reckoning includes demands for economic justice, almost all the energies of the identitarian left are mobilized in the service of psychic justice. This is why perceived verbal affronts are so often presented as equally as damaging as physical violence. And it helps explain why the same students who will shut down a university over a comment by a professor that they deem racist or anti-trans—while to be sure they will bemoan the economic hardships of the poor in the universities cities and towns in which they study—have never, to my knowledge, engaged in similar strikes, walkouts, let alone efforts to shut down their schools because of this (Yale

University is a perfect example of this: a mini-city state, rich as Qatar, around which is a mid-sized city, a majority of whose overwhelmingly non-white population live in poverty).

This is not to say that there is no truth to the old Feminist dictum that the personal is the political. But, in the Anglosphere at least, and, increasingly, in many other parts of the world as well, it is now clear that what this has come to mean is that the psychological is the political—a far more dubious claim given that despite the Woke-izing of therapy and, increasing, even of psychoanalysis—a recent book called *Decolonizing Therapy*[1] insists that, "All therapy is—and always has been—inherently political"—no matter how insistently you clothe the psyche's inherent subjectivity in the claim that all individual trauma is the productive of a collective trauma produced by oppression, above all by racism, the psyche will not be satisfied even if the Psych Department at the university will.

MY OLD MASTER, Ivan Illich, liked to say "We must rediscover the distinction between hope and expectation." This was at the beginning of the 1970s. In 2023, the idea that such a distinction is possible seems far-fetched. To hope is now understood as the beginning of a transaction, almost as if one were placing an order on Amazon, with just as firm an expectation that one's order will be fulfilled. Or to put it slightly different, a society that can no longer distinguish between its desires and its fate, the idea that what one hopes for will not sooner or later be actualized seems utterly intolerable, as if to say, "What is the point of hoping if such hoping is to be in vain?"

Part of this comes from the sense of entitlement that almost all citizens of rich societies share—even if they think of themselves as critics, stalwart in their resistance to their own societies. But a more important element is the medicalization of the idea of hope, a development that Illich, even in his obsession with the 'medical nemesis,' would have been taken aback by. Writing in 2021 in the blog of the Harvard Medical School, the Director of Psychiatry at Beth Israel Deaconess Medical Center's Berenson-Allen Center for Noninvasive Brain Stimulation, Adam P. Stern, wrote that, "Hope is an essential component of our well-being."[1] A year earlier, writing in the journal *Global Epidemiology*, Katelyn N. G. Long and her colleagues wrote that, given the,

> documented numerous positive associations between hope and subsequent health and well-being outcomes... public health researchers and practitioners [should put] their efforts on potentially trying to increase levels of

hope, and by possible extension, levels of health and well-being.[2]

On this account, not to be hopeful becomes a public health problem—one that public health practitioners need to find ways of countering, just as they would try to come up with ways of countering chronic disease, mental illness, or a poor diet, in a given population. Thus, as in so many other cases in rich, post-religious societies, a profound metaphysical idea is transformed into a medical necessity (social justice is another example of this transformation), whose attainment can be facilitated by public health professionals. Where such a view leads, is toward the recasting of a person's lack of hope as a medical condition. And, taken to its logical conclusion—but one that can easily be imagined—those without hope could be redefined as being possible health risks to the larger community. And the distance between that and Agamben 'state of exception' is a very short one.

I HAD BEEN UNAWARE OF the category of 'moral injury,' but it is, apparently, a commonplace term in the US medical world nowadays. A recently published study by doctors at the medical school of Duke University in collaboration with the Veterans' Administration distinguishes moral injury from mere burnout. "While 'burnout' is often used to describe the effects of ongoing stress in the workplace," the study's main author, Jason Nieuwsma declares in a press release,

> moral injury is used to describe the damage done to the conscience or identity of people who might witness, cause, or fail to prevent acts that go against their own moral standards. For example, with health care workers, this might entail them making choices or being part of situations that stray from their genuine commitment to healing.[1]

In what alternate universe do people imagine they will have the freedom not to even witness acts that go against their moral standards? It's hard enough in life not to betray them oneself. This is kindergarten utopianism, and its good intentions do not excuse it.

THE ORIGINAL MEDICAL DEFINITION of post-traumatic stress disorder (PTSD) was first defined by the American Psychiatric Association in 1980 in the third edition of its *Diagnostic and Statistical Manual of Mental Disorders* (commonly referred to as *DSM-III*) as as a catastrophic stressor that was outside the range of usual human experience. The framers of the original PTSD diagnosis had in mind events such as war, torture, rape, the Nazi Holocaust, the atomic bombings of Hiroshima and Nagasaki, natural disasters (such as earthquakes, hurricanes, and volcano eruptions), as well as human-made disasters (such as factory explosions, airplane crashes, and automobile accidents). On this account, traumatic events were clearly different what what psychiatrists and psychologists at that time thought of as the very painful 'stressors'—to use the term of art—that are part and parcel of all human lives, such as divorce, failure, rejection, serious illness, financial adversity, and the like. But, by the 2013, when DSM-V was published, a diagnosis of PTSD no longer required exposure to what were now referred to as "high magnitude catastrophic events"[1] of the original definition, such as combat exposure or violent rape, but also was also held to be warranted by so-called "lower magnitude events," such as learning that a family member had died, or witnessing a fight. In other words, not only were events that are a normal part of the vicissitudes of life and are experienced at some point between birth and death by almost everyone now included, but such events did not even have to be experienced directly.

This 'grade inflation' of what constitutes trauma is the new normal for the educational, public health, and psychoanalytic and therapeutic bureaucracies. The widely reported (and largely uncritically accepted) recent finding of a University of Alabama-Birmingham study published in the *Journal of the American Medical Association* (JAMA) that the incidence of PTSD on American university campuses had increased by 4.1% between 2017 and 2022 and now affected 7.5% of all US college students is an emblem of the current consensus. The authors of the study suggested that "the loss of loved ones during the pandemic" and "racial trauma" had contributed to the rise.[2] Another student went further, asserting that "in 2020–2021, >60% of students met criteria for one or more mental health problems, a nearly 50% increase from 2013,"[3] all of this in a context where, according to the 2021 National College Health Assessment of the American College Health Association, in terms of strictly physical health, 87% of college students described their health as "good, very good, or excellent."[4]

If these accounts are correct, then mental illness, rather than mental health, is increasingly becoming the norm among young people in the United States. But, in reality, what has occurred is a general lowering of the bar for what is and is not traumatizing. Given the increasing hegemony throughout the culture of a radical subjectivity in which, in the specific instance of mental health—as with that of gender identity—how one feels and how one is are asserted to be indistinguishable and, indeed, that it is a moral affront *not* to take any individual's self-description at face value, it could hardly be otherwise.

The radical expansion of the definition of what constitutes PTSD to include virtually any unhappy experience is simply the most extreme instance of this new abnormal—one that now bears the imprimatur of the American Psychological Association (APA). According to the APA, which at the end of 2023 issued a report entitled "Stress in America™ [sic] 2023: A Nation grappling with psychological impacts of collective trauma,"

> college students today are also juggling a dizzying array of challenges, from coursework, relationships, and adjustment to campus life to economic strain, social injustice, mass violence, and various forms of loss related to COVID-19.[5]

The reality, however, is that some of this 'dizzying array' such as 'coursework' and 'adjusting to campus life' has always been part and parcel of being a college student, while 'relationships' are simply part of being a human being. And, while it is certainly possible that today's college students are more conscious of social injustice and economic strain, they are no worse than in the past; indeed, arguably at least, they are better. In fact, the only element in the APA's menu of challenges that can indeed be argued to be traumatic in the sense of the original definition of PTSD as a tragedy or shock outside the range of normal human experience, is the COVID pandemic.

The likelier explanation for the mental health crisis of the young is that it is a crisis of expectations. And, if their response often seems like a form of collective hysteria, it is not one for which they can fairly be held responsible. To the contrary, they are the victims of the fusion of the 'Wellness' culture that has so dominated the American imagination for so many decades and, contrary to the assumptions of some critics, owes nothing to identitarian politics and Woke, with the language of rights that is at the root of these expectations of serenity and psychic well-being which no other generation throughout human history in the USA or anywhere else has ever imagined to be owed to them. The result has, indeed, been a collective psychological disaster, just not the one that the psychologists think it is. What has really happened is that the young have been sold a bill of goods: the fraudulent promise that their desires *should be* their fates.

THE TRIUMPH OF THE TRAUMATIC could not exist without the parallel Triumph of the Histrionic. For, outside the theater and the opera, the histrionic used to be largely the monopoly of politicians and preachers—in particular of the populist and totalitarian kind. In our age, however, the histrionic has become a mass phenomenon. That it is the lifeblood of social media should be obvious, since in cyberspace hyperbole rules, be it of the political or of the pop cultural sort—that is, whether focused on Gaza or on Taylor Swift. But, to blame social media for this is nothing more than the proverbial shooting of the messenger. For, the contemporary desire of so many in Western society (and, increasingly, in non-Western societies as well) to recast themselves virtually at will can only be credible in the context of the performative. This is why Judith Butler's work has been so influential and why, despite its sticky sentimentalities, it is so important: it has popularized the idea that there are no fixed identities but, instead, various performances, some repressive, others emancipatory. It is Shakespeare's "All the world's a stage," but without Shakespeare's realism about inevitable decline and final oblivion, or his cold realism about people being merely players awaiting their exits. In the sunny uplands of Butler's vision, each individual is not a 'mere' anything, but rather always the star of the show, and with no producer or casting director needed. To the contrary, each individual is the "actor-manager," as my father put it in *The Triumph of the Therapeutic*, "of his own infinitely changeable identities." By comparison, Andy Warhol's line that we would all be famous for fifteen minutes seems the height of sober caution. He did not see that people wanted more than to be famous, more than to able to communicate directly with their gods; instead, they wanted to be able to define themselves at will, which, when you think about it, is nothing short of a way of conferring godlike powers to oneself.

The move is radical: from 'truth' to 'my truth,' and from the vicissitudes of fate to the supremacy of desire. Fate, though, will have the last word; it always has, and it always will. If on nothing else, on that we can depend.

NOTES

Unsurprisingly, the destruction… **[p. 4]**

1 T. S. Eliot, "Tradition and the Individual Talent," in T. S. Eliot, *Selected Essays* (London: Faber and Faber, 1932).

2 Daniel Bell, *The Cultural Contradictions of Capitalism* (New York: Basic Books, 1976).

3 Ibid.

4 Ibid.

In 1997, the social critic… **[p. 14]**

1 See Thomas Frank, "Why Johnny Can't Dissent," in Stephen Duncombe, *Cultural Resistance Reader* (London: Verso, 2002).

2 David Rieff, "Multiculturalism's Silent Partner," *Harper's Magazine* (Aug 1993).

3 David Gelles, "How Environmentally Conscious Investing Became a Target of Conservatives," *The New York Times*, (28 Feb 2023).

4 Breck Dumas, "Former Levi's Exec Says 'Woke Ca-pi-talism' Has Taken Over Corporate Boardrooms," *Fox Business*, (25 Oct 2022).

5 'Wesley Yang on The Successor Ideology,' The Dishcast with Andrew Sullivan, *The Weekly Dish*.

6 Interestingly, Yang proposes that during the same period a parallel 'long march' was taking place on the right with the founding of the Federalist Society that would blaze the trail of a new conservative legal movement.

[7] 'The Successor Ideology and the Threat to Our Freedoms,' Opinion: Free Expression, *WSJ Podcasts*, (13 June 2022).

[8] Thomas Frank, Ibid.

[9] See <https://x.com/tribunaltweets/status/1569286459386957825>.

[10] See <https://x.com/laynemorgan/status/830078635306414082>.

[11] Amia Srinivasan, "Does Anyone Have The Right to Sex?" *London Review of Books*, 40/6, (22 Mar 2018).

[12] Thomas Frank, Ibid.

[13] Michael Hammer and James Champy, *Reengineering the Corporation: A Manifesto for Business Revolution* (New York: HarperCollins, 1993).

[14] The tweet has since been taken down.

[15] Thomas Frank, Ibid.

[16] Sheila McClear, "Disney Prez of Entertainment Wants 50 Percent of All Characters Gay or 'Underrepresented,'" *Los Angeles Magazine*, (30 Mar 2022).

[17] Thomas Frank, Ibid.

There is an old joke... **[p. 29]**

[1] Fikile Nxumalo and Wanja Gitari, "Introduction to the Special Theme on Responding to Anti-Blackness in Science, Mathematics, Technology and STEM Education," *Canadian Journal of Science, Mathematics and Technology Education = Revue canadienne de l'enseignement des sciences, des mathematiques et de la technologie*, (21 Feb 2021).

[2] See Fidel Castro's speech to intellectuals on 30 June 1961, <http://lanic.utexas.edu/project/castro/db/1961/19610630.html>.

On a podcast called "All-In"... **[p. 31]**

[1] Ananda Macias, "Billionaire investor Chamath Palihapitiya says 'nobody cares' about Uyghur genocide in China," *CNBC*, (19 Jan 2022).

[2] See <https://x.com/WarriorsPR/status/1483179382134898690?s=20>.

[3] See <https://x.com/chamath/status/1483228175391866881/photo/1>.

[4] Ananda Macias, Ibid.

V-Dem is a Swedish think tank... **[p. 34]**

[1] See <https://freedomhouse.org/about-us>.

[2] See <https://www.v-dem.net/our-work/research-programs/case-for-democracy/>.

[3] See V-Dem Institute's "Democracy Report 2023: Defiance in the Face of Autocratization" <https://www.v-dem.net/documents/29/V-dem_democracyreport2023_lowres.pdf>.

[4] Samuel Moyn, "Hype for the Best," *The New Republic*, (19 Mar 2018).

[5] "'Democracy isn't Coca-Cola': Beijing says US shouldn't assume that representative government 'tastes' the same all over the world," CubaSí, (24 Apr 2021).

[6] See *Rest of World* <https://restofworld.org>.

[7] Jillian Godsil, "Andy Tian Interview, CEO Of The Fastest Selling ICO In Asia, $30 Million Raised In 1 Minute!," *CryptoCoin.News*, (22 Dec 2017).

[8] Peter Guest, "Why China is pioneering the next generation of social media," *Rest of World*, (21 Apr 2021).

The novelist and critic... **[p. 40]**

[1] See <https://x.com/_ryanruby>.

[2] Ibid.

The Woke vision… **[p. 44]**

[1] See "Apply to The New York Times Diverse Crossword Constructor Fellowship" <https://www.nytimes.com/2022/10/24/crosswords/apply-to-the-new-york-times-diverse-crossword-constructor-fellowship.html>.

It should, by now… **[p. 45]**

[1] Vasconcelos uses the word 'raza,' which can mean both people and race. See <https://www.neocrotalic.com/post/revolutionizing-mexican-art-jose-vasconcelos-national-identity>.

By now, to observe… **[p. 47]**

[1] Stan Grant, "To Understand China You Need to Understand Whiteness, Yet it's Missing From The Conversation," *ABC News*, (15 Oct 2022).

These two famous quotations… **[p. 53]**

[1] Antonio Gramsci, *Prison Notebooks*, (New York: Columbia University Press, 2011).

[2] Giuseppe Tomasi Di Lampedusa, *The Leopard*, (New York: Pantheon, 1991).

[3] Amber Murrey and Patricia Daley, *Learning Disobedience: Decolonizing Development Studies* (London: Pluto Press, 2023).

For capitalism… **[p. 58]**

[1] American Medical Association and Association of American Medical Colleges, *Advancing Health Equity: Guide on Language, Narrative and Concepts*, (2021), <ama-assn.org/equity-guide>.

[2] "Epic Fail For National Nurses Week," *EmpoweredNurses.org*, (13 May 2021).

[3] Adolph Reed, Jr., "The Uses of Affirmative Action," *The Nation*, (9 Aug 2023).

Walter Benjamin famously said... **[p. 63]**

[1] Arthur Miller, "The Year It Came Apart," *New York Magazine*, (30 Dec 1974–6 Jan 1975).

[2] V. I. Lenin, *Collected Works* (Moscow: Progress Publishers, 1964), Vol. XXXI.

To dismiss Woke as mere... **[p. 66]**

[1] Giverny Masso, "Arts Council: Relevance not Excellence Will Be New Litmus Test for Funding," *The Stage*, (8 Apr 2019).

[2] John Berry, "The Arts Council Is Harming The Cultural Organisations It Should Help." *Prospect*, (15 Nov 2022).

One of the most striking... **[p. 70]**

[1] Robin DiAngelo, *Nice Racism: How Progressive White People Perpetuate Racial Harm* (Boston: Beacon Press, 2021).

[2] Ibid.

Duke University Press... **[p. 77]**

[1] Leigh Claire La Berge, *Marx for Cats* (Durham, NC: Duke University Press, 2023).

[2] All passages are from Leigh Claire La Berge, "Marx for Cats," *Dilettante Army* <https://dilettantearmy.com/articles/marx-for-cats>.

[3] Ibid.

The two most powerful elements... **[p. 79]**

[1] Deborah Cohan, "Racist Like Me–Call to Self-Reflection

and Action for White Physicians," *New England Journal of Medicine*, (29 Feb 2019).

Blake Bailey, the author of... **[p. 84]**

[1] Ramon Antonio Vargas, "Blake Bailey, Biographer Accused of Harassment and Rape, to Publish Memoir," *The Guardian* (27 Jul 2022).

[2] Ramon Antonio Vargas, "Author Blake Bailey Accused of Abusing ex-Lusher Students' Trust For Sex; Denies Illegal Conduct," *Nola* (21 Apr 2021).

[3] Laura Miller, "'He Didn't Care if he Destroyed Himself as Long as he Hurt You': The Sad, Disturbing Case of Ed Champion," *Salon* (30 Sep 2014).

[4] See <http://www.edrants.com/about/>.

[5] Sian Cain "Publisher Halts Philip Roth Book Amid Sexual Abuse Claims Against Biographer," *The Guardian*, (21 Apr 2021).

[6] Christie D'Zurilla, "Philip Roth Biographer Blake Bailey Dropped by Agent Over 'Grooming' Allegations," *Los Angeles Times*, (20 Apr 2021).

[7] See <https://fkks.com/news/a-moral-dilemma-morals-clauses-in-endorsement-contracts>.

The disclosure that the works... **[p. 89]**

[1] Ed Cumming, Abigail Buchanan, Genevieve Holl-Allen, "The Rewriting of Roald Dahl," *The Telegraph*, (24 Feb 2023).

[2] Kat Eschner, "The Bowdlers Wanted to Clean Up Shakespeare, Not Become a Byword for Censorship," *Smithsonian Magazine*, (11 Jul 2017).

[3] See Preface to the First Edition in Thomas Bowdler, *The Family Shakespeare In One Volume* (London: Longman, Brown, Green, and Longmans, 1847).

[4] Ibid.

[5] Hayden Vernon, "Roald Dahl Books Rewritten to Remove Language Deemed Offensive," *The Guardian*, (18 Feb 2023).

[6] Ibid.

[7] Sian Bayley, "Puffin Defends 'Minimal' Changes Made to Roald Dahl's Children's Books," *The Bookseller*, (22 Feb 2023).

[8] Seth Abramovitch, "Roald Dahl Publisher Bends to Controversy, Will Release 'Classic' Version of Controversial Kids' Books," *The Hollywood Reporter*, (24 Feb 2023).

[9] Ibid.

[10] Sian Bayley, Ibid.

[11] Cumming, Buchanan, Holl-Allen, Ibid.

[12] Ibid.

[13] Sian Bayley, Ibid.

[14] Ibid.

[15] Ibid.

[16] Roger Scruton, "Kitsch and the Modern Predicament," *City Journal*, (Winter 1999).

Robert Hughes wrote that... **[p. 100]**

[1] Robert Hughes, "Art, Morals, and Politics," *The New York Review*, (23 Apr 1992).

It should be obvious by now... **[p. 101]**

[1] Abram Tertz (pseudonym for Andrei Sinyavsky), *The Trial Begins and On Socialist Realism* (New York: Vintage Books, 1960).

The Guardian reports... **[p. 104]**

[1] Eva Corlett, "New Zealand Pulls Funding For School

Shakespeare Festival, Citing 'Canon of Imperialism,'" *The Guardian* (14 Oct 2022).

[2] Ibid.

[3] Baz Macdonald, "Thou Art 'Boring as Shit,'" *Re:News*, (12 Oct 2022).

[4] See <https://www.neocrotalic.com/post/revolutionizing-mexican-art-jose-vasconcelos-national-identity>.

Writers are increasingly... **[p. 107]**

[1] Monisha Rajesh, "Pointing Out Racism in Books is Not an 'Attack' – It's a Call For Industry Reform," *The Guardian*, (13 Aug 2021).

[2] Tara Tobler, "Lessons from Clanchy," *The Bookseller*, (1 Oct 2021).

[3] Ibid.

It is reported that... **[p. 110]**

[1] Chris Hastings, "Wokery Beyond Parody Because University Slaps a TRIGGER Warning on George Orwell's 1984 as it Contains 'Explicit Material' Which Some Students May Find 'Offensive and Upsetting,'" *Daily Mail*, (22 Jan 2022).

Trigger warnings have... **[p. 112]**

[1] See <https://www.nimh.nih.gov/health/topics/post-traumatic-stress-disorder-ptsd>.

[2] Brett Milano, "Should hateful speech be regulated on campus?", *The Harvard Gazette*, (24 Feb 2020).

[3] See <https://dictionary.apa.org/intergenerational-trauma>.

[4] Brendan Pierson, "California Law Aiming to Curb COVID Misinformation Blocked by Judge," *Reuters*, (26 Jan 2023). This law has been challenged in the

courts on free speech grounds and is currently stayed.

[5] See <https://system.suny.edu/odei/>.

[6] Sometimes even a single student, such as the one at Hamline University who declared herself the victim of Islamophobia because an art history teacher at the institution had showed her class an image from a fourteenth century Persian manuscript representing the Prophet Mohammed.

To try to parse the rise... **[p. 117]**

[1] Kai Johnson, Tanika Lynch, Elizabeth Monroe, and Tracey Wang, "Our Identities Matter in Core Classrooms," *Columbia Spectator*, (30 Apr 2015).

[2] Eliana Dockterman, "Columbia Undergrads Say Greek Mythology Needs a 'Trigger Warning,'" *TIME*, (15 May 2015).

[3] Brian Duignan, "Trigger Warnings on Campus," *Britannica*, <https://www.britannica.com/story/trigger-warnings-on-campus>.

[4] Colleen Flaherty, "Trigger Unhappy," *Inside Higher Ed*, (13 Apr 2014).

[5] Maya Jaggi, "Storyteller of the Savannah," *The Guardian*, (18 Nov 2000).

[6] Colleen Flaherty, Ibid.

[7] Ibid.

[8] Ibid.

[9] Jeannie Suk Gersen, "What If Trigger Warnings Don't Work," *The New Yorker*, (28 Dec 2021).

[10] Katie McKay, "Trigger warnings have gone too far," *The Glasgow Guardian*, (27 Mar 2023).

[11] Blake Mauro, "University Puts Trigger Warning on Hemingway's 'Old Man And The Sea': 'Graphic Fishing Scenes,'" *The College Fix*, (12 Jul 2023).

[12] Katie McKay, Ibid.

[13] See <https://www.bbfc.co.uk/about-classification/classification-guidelines>.

[14] Craig Simpson, "James Joyce's Ulysses Issued With Trigger Warning After it is Deemed 'Offensive' to Modern Students," *The Telegraph*, (2 Feb 2023).

[15] See <https://x.com/keatsandchapman>.

The Oracle, *the student newspaper…* **[p. 126]**

[1] Kenan Malik, "An Art Treasure Long Cherished by Muslims is Deemed Offensive. But to Whom?", *The Guardian*, (8 Jan 2023).

[2] Eugene Voloch, "Hamline Student Newspaper (the Oracle) Removed Published Defense of Lecturer Who Showed Painting of Muhammad," *Reason*, (26 Dec 2022).

The Associated Press Stylebook… **[p. 128]**

[1] See <https://www.localinstitutes.cii.co.uk/media/15671/inclusive-language-guidelines.pdf>.

[2] Susan D'Agostino, "Amid Backlash, Stanford Pulls 'Harmful Language' List," *Inside Higher Ed*, (10 Jan 2023).

[3] See <https://library.usfca.edu/harmful-language-statement>.

[4] See <https://x.com/AP/status/1618886923828748288?lang=en>.

[5] Nicolas Camut, "Don't Say 'The French' as it's Offensive, AP Says," *Politico*, (27 Jan 2023).

[6] See <https://x.com/APStylebook/status/1619005157508845568?lang=en>.

For all the mockery… **[p. 133]**

1 See <https://www.thesaurus.com/e/writing/person-first-vs-identity-first-language/>.

2 Sheila McClear, "Stanford Releases 'Harmful Language' List of Hurtful Words to Eliminate," *Los Angeles Magazine.*

3 "PETA says these phrases are comparable to racism and homophobia," *ABC Action News*, (5 Dec 2018).

4 Amy B. Wang, "PETA Wants to Change 'Anti-animal' Sayings, But the Internet Thinks They're Feeding a Fed Horse," *The Washington Post*, (6 Dec 2018).

5 See <https://www.merriam-webster.com/wordplay/what-is-the-new-meaning-of-bandwidth>.

The art world and the world… **[p. 139]**

1 Maximilíano Durón, "Cape Town–Based Curator Khanyisile Mbongwa to Organize 2023 Liverpool Biennial," *ArtNews*, (26 Jan 2022).

Milan Kundera's definition… **[p. 141]**

1 Milan Kundera, *The Unbearable Lightness of Being*, (London: Faber and Faber, 1999).

The 2023 New Year celebrations… **[p. 142]**

1 See <https://www.sydneynewyearseve.com/fireworks/>.

2 Charley Adams & Chris Giles, "New year: Tributes to Late Queen as Fireworks Welcome in 2023," *BBC*, (1 Jan 2023), The compatibility of the Ukrainian case with LGBT rights is actually very hard to overstate. On Twitter, for example it is now commonplace to find accounts displaying only two flags: the Pride rainbow and the blue and yellow of Ukraine. Given that Putin has described the war on a number of occasions as being in

part a war to protect Russia's anti-woke values, and the way anti-woke hysteria is commonly deployed on Russian television, this shouldn't come as a surprise.

[3] See <https://x.com/PaulEmbery>.

[4] Ibid.

Although it was genuinely… **[p. 145]**

[1] Aldous Huxley, *Brave New World*, (London: Vintage, 1932).

Sympathy for Hal… **[p. 149]**

[1] Gerrit De Vynck and Nitasha Tiku, "Google Takes Down Gemini AI Image Generator. Here's What You Need to Know," *The Washington Post*, (23 Feb 2024).

[2] Nico Grant, "Google Chatbot's A.I. Images Put People of Color in Nazi-Era Uniforms," *The New York Times*, (22 Feb 2024).

[3] Ibid.

[4] Miles Klee, "Blue Checks Attack Google's 'Woke' AI Art While Admiring Hitler's Paintings," *Rolling Stone*, (23 Feb 2024).

[5] See <https://twitter.com/NateSilver538/status/1761800684272308302>.

[6] Noor Al-Sibai, "Google Chatbot Refused to Say Whether Elon Musk Is Better Than Adolf Hitler," *Futurism*, (26 Feb 2024).

One of the more astonishing… **[p. 156]**

[1] Cheryl I. Harris, "Whiteness as Property," *Harvard Law Review*, (10 Jun 1993), <https://harvardlawreview.org/print/no-volume/whiteness-as-property/>.

[2] An aside: the Qing Dynasty began in 1644, that is, twenty-five years after the founding grounded in

slavery that the 1619 Project proposes. It seems doubtful the Qing-era idea of property was somehow a subset of the American experience. But that's just what the argument of people like Harris do: misread the American experience into one that is definitional of private property itself.

[3] Sofia Leung, "Whiteness as Collections," (30 Sep 2019), <https://www.sofiayleung.com/thoughts/whiteness-as-collections>.

The website MedPage Today... **[p. 159]**

[1] Robert M. McLean and Douglas M. DeLong, "Op-Ed: An Open Letter to Our Fellow White Male Physicians," *MedPage Today*, (23 Apr 2021).

[2] Ibid.

[3] See <https://www.aamc.org/data-reports/workforce/data/figure-13-percentage-us-medical-school-graduates-race-ethnicity-alone-academic-year-2018-2019>.

[4] See <https://en.wikipedia.org/wiki/Demographics_of_the_United_States>.

[5] See <https://www.census.gov/data/tables/time-series/demo/popest/2010s-state-detail.html>.

[6] See <https://www.schooldigger.com/go/CA/schools/3441005643/school.aspx?>.

Senator Elizabeth Warren... **[p. 167]**

[1] A detail: the binary of white/people of color could not, as it does in Sen. Warren's bill, include Asian-Americans (to the extent that dubious term means anything at all) were economic criteria of racial harm the sole ones being applied.

[2] See <https://www.congress.gov/bill/117th-congress/senate-bill/162/text>.

The Student Union of… **[p. 168]**

[1] Louisa Clarence-Smith, "White students banned from Black History Month events at Westminster University," *The Telegraph*, (7 Oct 2022).

[2] All references drawn from "Cambridge Professor Priyamvada Gopal Tweets 'White Lives Don't Matter,' Follows It Up With 'Abolish Brahmins And Upper Castes,'" *Swarajya*, (25 Jun 2020), <https://swarajyamag.com/insta/cambridge-professor-priyamvada-gopal-tweets-white-lives-dont-matter-follows-it-up-with-abolish-brahmins-and-upper-castes>.

The Journal Composition Studies… **[p. 170]**

[1] See <https://compstudiesjournal.com>.

[2] See <https://compstudiesjournal.com/a-guide-for-anti-racist-scholarly-reviewing-practices-at-composition-studies>.

There is an excellent piece… **[p. 172]**

[1] Amna Khalid and Jeffrey Aaron Snyder, "Yes, DEI, Can Erode Academic Freedom. Let's Not Pretend Otherwise," *The Chronicle of Higher Education*, (6 Feb 2023).

[2] Ibid.

The Academic Senate… **[p. 176]**

[1] See <https:/www.asccc.org>.

[2] See <https://www.asccc.org/sites/default/files/CCC_DEI-in-Curriculum_Model_Principles_and_Practices_June_2022.pdf>.

To disagree is to traumatize… **[p. 177]**

[1] See "Task Force Report on Equity and Anti-Racism

in Research," <https://research.ucsf.edu/task-force-report-equity-and-anti-racism-research>.

[2] Ibid.

[3] Ibid.

[4] Ibid.

A society in moral free fall... **[p. 180]**

[1] Jerry A. Coyne and Luana S. Maroja, "The Ideological Subversion of Biology," *Skeptical Inquirer*, 47/4, (Jul/Aug 2023).

[2] Max Weber, "Science as a Vocation," in H. H. Gerth and C. Wright Mills (trans. and ed.), *From Max Weber: Essays in Sociology*, (New York: Oxford University Press, 1946).

[3] See "Attorney General Bonta Releases Inaugural State of Pride Report in Honor of LGBTQ+ Pride Month," <https://oag.ca.gov/news/press-releases/attorney-general-bonta-releases-inaugural-state-pride-report-honor-lgbtq-pride>.

[4] See <https://www.songfacts.com/lyrics/ray-stevens/everything-is-beautiful>.

[5] Philip Rieff, *The Triumph of the Therapeutic: Uses of Faith After Freud*, (Wilmington, DE: Intercollegiate Studies Institute, 2006).

Having been traumatized... **[p. 183]**

[1] Cody Dailey, "Addressing Trauma in the College Essay," IACAC, (29 Oct 2020), <https://www.iacac.org/2020/10/addressing-trauma-in-the-college-essay/>.

Therapeutic language has... **[p. 184]**

[1] Amy Simonson, "Florida bill to shield people from feeling 'discomfort' over historic actions by their race,

nationality or gender approved by Senate committee," *CNN*, (19 Jan 2022), <https://edition.cnn.com/2022/01/19/us/florida-education-critical-race-theory-bill/index.html>.

The Triumph of the Traumatic… **[p. 186]**

[1] See <https://www.lemkininstitute.com/statements-new-page/statement-on-the-genocidal-nature-of-the-gender-critical-movement's-ideology-and-practice>.

[2] See <https://drdevika.wordpress.com/2016/11/12/i-a-richards-practical-criticism/>.

Utopia and revolution… **[p. 188]**

[1] See "Children and gender identity: Supporting your child," <https://www.mayoclinic.org/healthy-lifestyle/childrens-health/in-depth/children-and-gender-identity/art-20266811>.

[2] Amanda D'Ambrosio, "Here's How Ob/Gyns Can Create Gender-Affirming Environments," *MedPage Today*, (10 Feb 2022).

[3] See "It's time for real transgender representation in NYC government," *Daily News*, (20 Feb 2022).

[4] Judith Thurman, *Cleopatra's Nose*, (New York: MacMillan, 2007).

In a world where there is… **[p. 193]**

[1] Shaul Bar-Haim, "Becoming a Peter Pan: Omnipotence, Dependency and the Ferenczian Child," <https://pubmed.ncbi.nlm.nih.gov/25720781/>.

[2] Theodor Adorno, *Minima Moralia: Reflections from Damaged Life*, (London: Verso Books, 2020).

[3] See <https://www.themarginalian.org/2015/09/11/theodor-adorno-work-pleasure-gadgeteering/>.

[4] See <https://x.com/grassfay>.

A Canadian social worker… **[p. 196]**

[1] See <https://www.kaedenseburn.com>.

[2] A screenshot of the document is posted on Chanel Pfahl's X feed <https://x.com/ChanLPfa>.

[3] See <https://www.kaedenseburn.com>.

[4] Ibid.

[5] Ibid.

[6] The French title, *L'Enfant et la vie familiale sous l'Ancien Régime* [*The Child and Family Life Under the Ancient Régime*], is more informative.

[7] Anastasia Ulanowicz, "Philippe Ariès," <https://www.representingchildhood.pitt.edu/pdf/aries.pdf>.

The trans movement's rupture… **[p. 201]**

[1] Natalia Mehlman Petrzela, "When Wellness Was Weird," Well + Good, (14 Jul 2015).

[2] See <https://www.statista.com/statistics/270720/market-size-of-the-wellness-industry-by-segment/>.

It used to be a psychiatric… **[p. 207]**

[1] Jennifer Mullan, *Decolonizing Therapy: Oppression, Historical Trauma, and Politicizing Your Practice*, (New York: W. W. Norton & Company, 2023).

My old master… **[p. 209]**

[1] Adam P. Stern, "Hope: Why it matters," *Harvard Health Blog*, (16 Jul 2021).

[2] Katelyn N. G. Long, Eric S. Kim, Ying Chen, Matthew F. Wilson, Everett L. Worthington Jr., Tyler J. VanderWeele, "The Role of Hope in Subsequent Health and Well-Being For Older Adults: An Outcome-Wide

Longitudinal Approach," *Global Epidemiology*, 2, (Nov 2020).

I had been unaware of... **[p. 211]**

[1] Sarah Avery, "Indications of Moral Injury Similar between Combat Veterans, COVID-19 Health Care Workers," Duke Health News & Media, (5 Apr 2022).

The original medical definition... **[p. 212]**

[1] Diagnostic and Statistical Manual of Mental Disorders, Text Revision DSM-5-TR, (Washington, DC: American Psychiatric Association, 2022).

[2] Adam Pope, "PTSD and ASD Diagnoses Rise Among College Dtudents, New UAB Research Shows," *UAB News*, (24 Jun 2024).

[3] Ibid.

[4] See <https://www.uhs.wisc.edu/prevention/ncha2021>.

[5] See <https://www.apa.org/news/press/releases/2023/11/psychological-impacts-collective-trauma>.

David Rieff is a journalist, cultural critic, essayist, and policy analyst. Beginning in the 1990s, he has reported on wars and humanitarian crises from Bosnia through Rwanda and the Democratic Republic of Congo, Sierra Leone, Liberia, Israel-Palestine, and Iraq and Afghanistan, to Ukraine today. In books including *Slaughterhouse: Bosnia and the Fair of the West*, *At the Point of a Gun: Democratic Dreams and Armed Intervention*, *A Bed for the Night: Humanitarianism in Crisis*, and *The Reproach of Hunger: Food, Justice and Money in the 21st Century*, Rieff anatomized the liberal pieties of our age: humanitarian action, the human rights movement, and the United Nations system. He has also written on international migration, contemporary Latin America, and, most recently, on the uses and abuses of historical memory in his book *In Praise of Forgetting: Historical Memory and its Ironies*.